EUROPEAN DIME NOVEL ART

compiled by Joseph A. Lovece

DIME NOVEL COVER SPECIAL EDITION 2

Also by the author:

The Steam Man of the West

The Road Home

The Flying Prairie Schooner

The Transatlantic Race

Dime Novel Cover:

Denver Doll the Detective Queen

Six Weeks in the Moon

Hank Hound, the Crescent City Detective

Sherlock Holmes Versus Jack the Ripper

Hercules, the Dumb Destroyer

Night Hawk

Sexton Blake: The Missing Millionaire

Lord Lister, known as Raffles, Master Thief

The Witch Hunter's Wards

Fantastic, Amazing and Beautiful Dime Novel Art

Introduction

From the beginning of the 20th century continental European publishers began flooding the markets with popular literature, including reprints of American dime novels and British penny dreadful, and original serial parts. The titles were translated across boundaries, so that the same novel with the original cover may appear simultaneously in Germany and France, for example.

Among the most popular titles were reprints of Buffalo Bill and Nick Carter from the U.S.A., and Claude Duval and Dick Turpin from England. In addition, many series were based in the American Old West, including the New Leatherstocking (Germany), Dick Norton, Jim Bradee. and Sitting Bull (Spain),

4

Les Chefs Indiens Célèbres (France); and detective stories based in London (Lord Lister aka Raffles, Germany). Original unlicensed stories also appeared, such as Sherlock Holmes.

Unlike their counterparts in America, European artists were much more likely to sign their work. Names like Luis Palao, Donaz, and T. Scarpelli reach us across through time.

For this edition title translations are provided, as well as bibliographic information when available, including original American edition sources.

Sitting Bull El Ultimo Sioux (The Last Sioux) No. 19, first series, circa 1912. El Salteador de Diligencias (The Assaulter of Proceedings), anonymous.

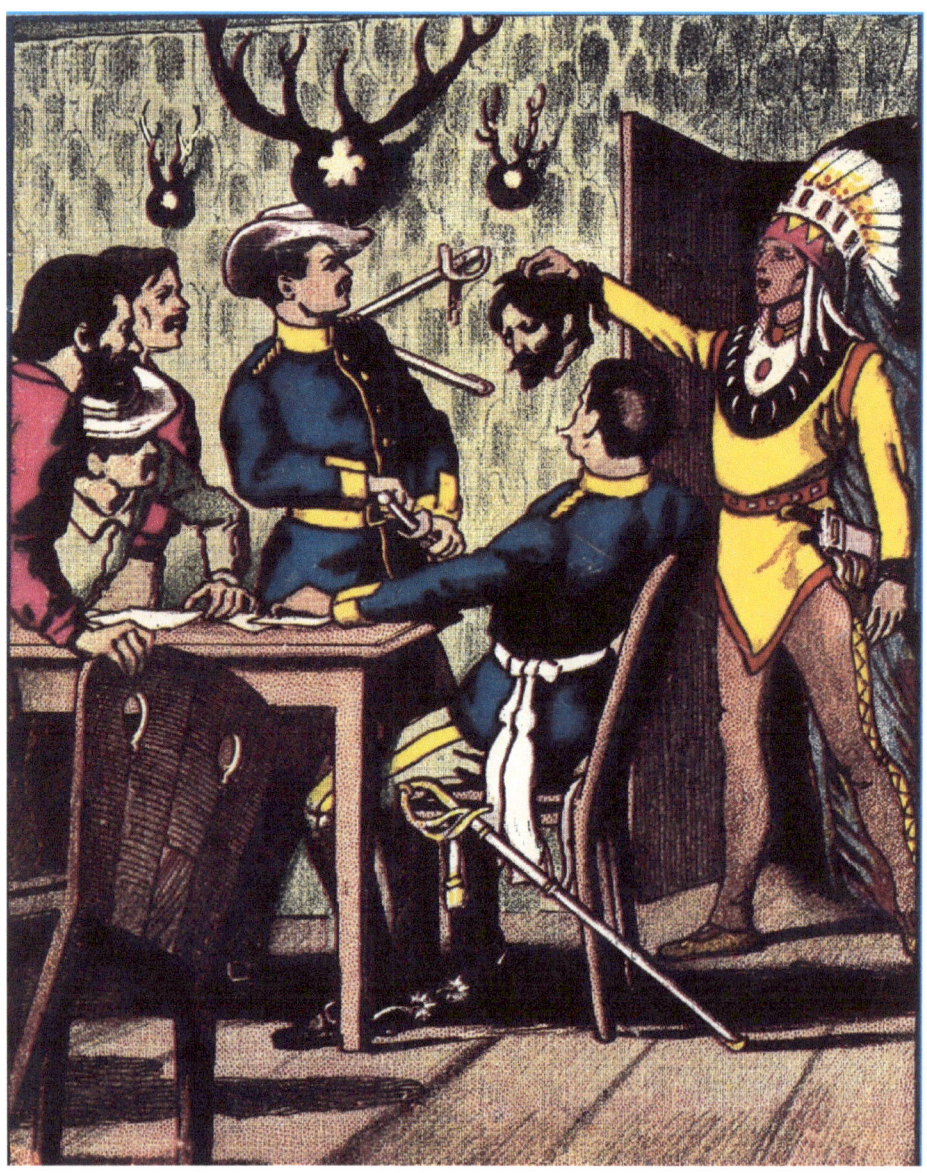

Los Cinco Invencibles (The Five Invincibles) No. 6, circa 1931. La Victima de un Traidor (The Traitor's Victim), anonymous but credited to Antonio Oller Bertran. Cover by Masgoumiery Daniel Pena (signed Niel).

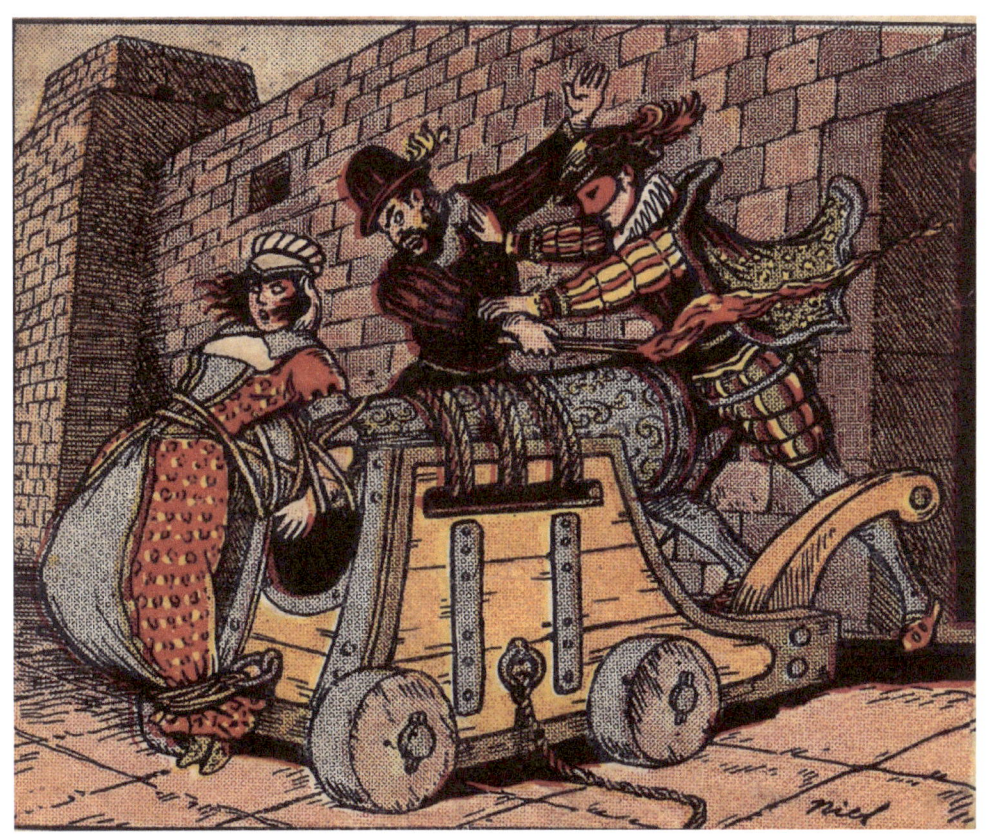

Journal des Voyages et des Aventures de Terre et de Mer (The Journal of Travel and Adventures on Land and Sea) Vol. 2 No. 220 (No. 1232), February 17, 1901. Fantaisie d'Astronome A la Surface de Mars (Astronomical Fantasy the Surface of Mars) by Wilfrid de Ponvielle.

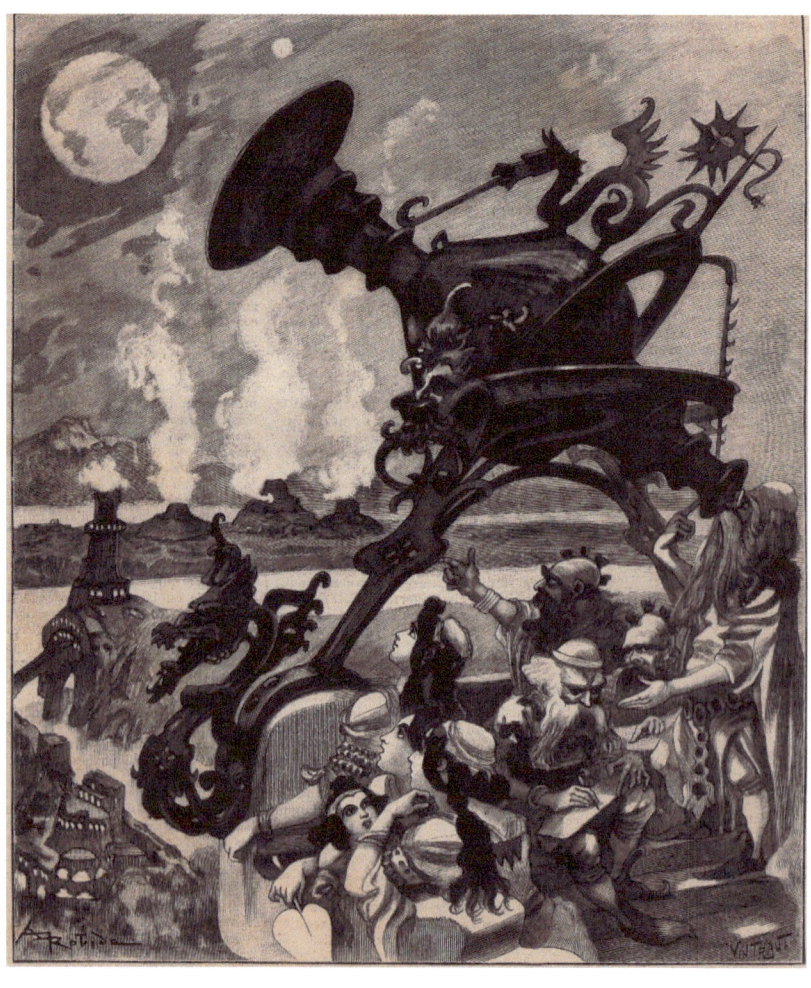

Pieles Rojas Contra Blancos (Red Skins Versus Whites) No. 14, circa 1915. El Bautismo de Sangre en el Fuerte William-Henry (The Baptism of Blood of Fort William-Henry). Spanish reprint of French dime novel *Les Chefs Indiens Célèbres* No. 14, 1909.

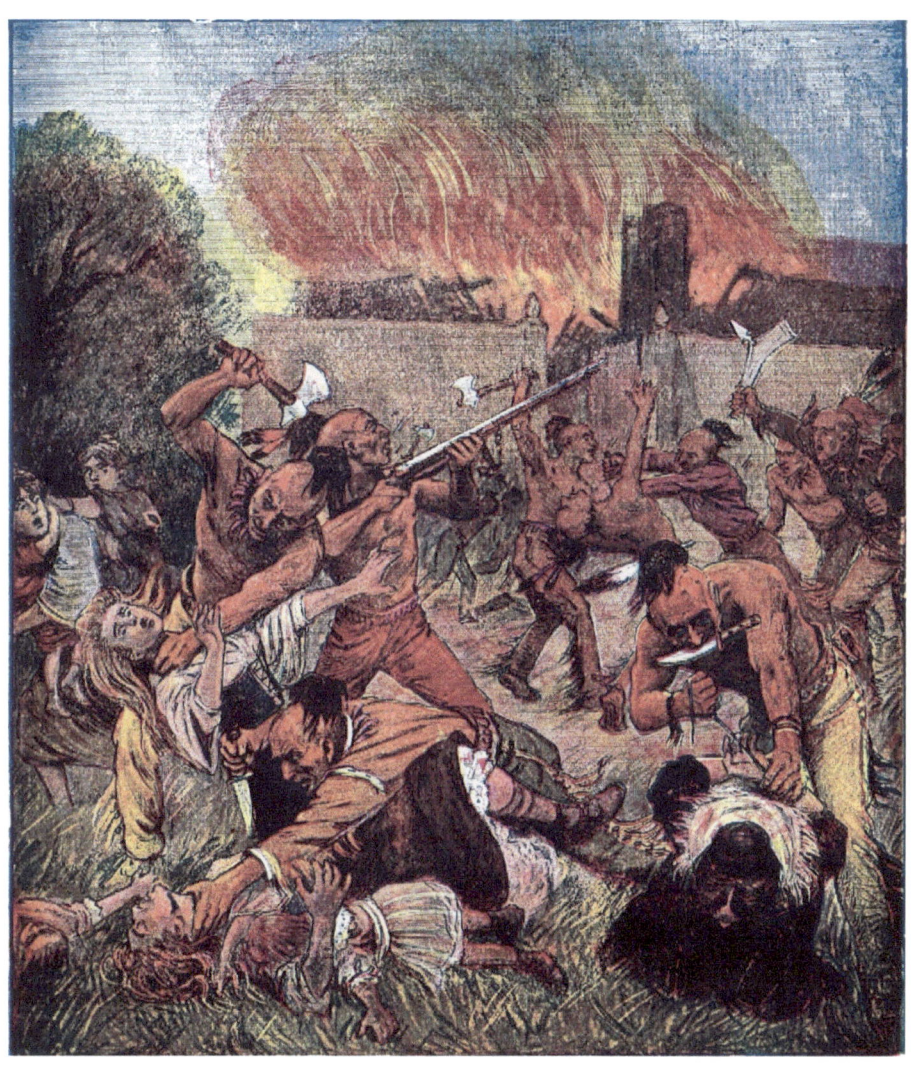

El Aventurero Millonario No. 8, 1931. El Tango de la Muerte (The Tango of Death), anonymous (Hugo Reyd?). "Exciting adventures of an orphan millionaire that invests his fortune into risky ventures protecting victims of the powerful and combating evil."

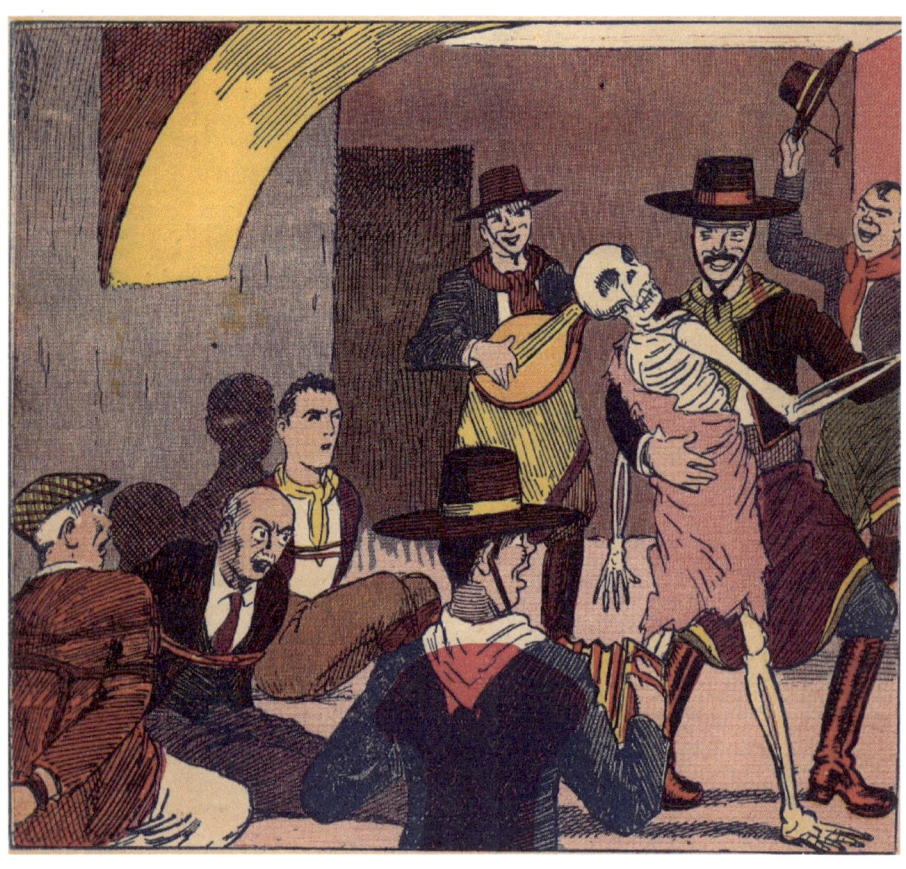

Buffalo Bill Aventuras Emocionantes No. 43, 1924. Los Fumadores de Opio (The Opium Smokers), anonymous. New cover by Luis Palao. Reprint of *Buffalo Bill Stories* No. 447, Buffalo Bill and the Heathen Chinee or the Missing Witness. Also reprinted in French *Buffalo Bill* No. 73, 1930, with the original cover.

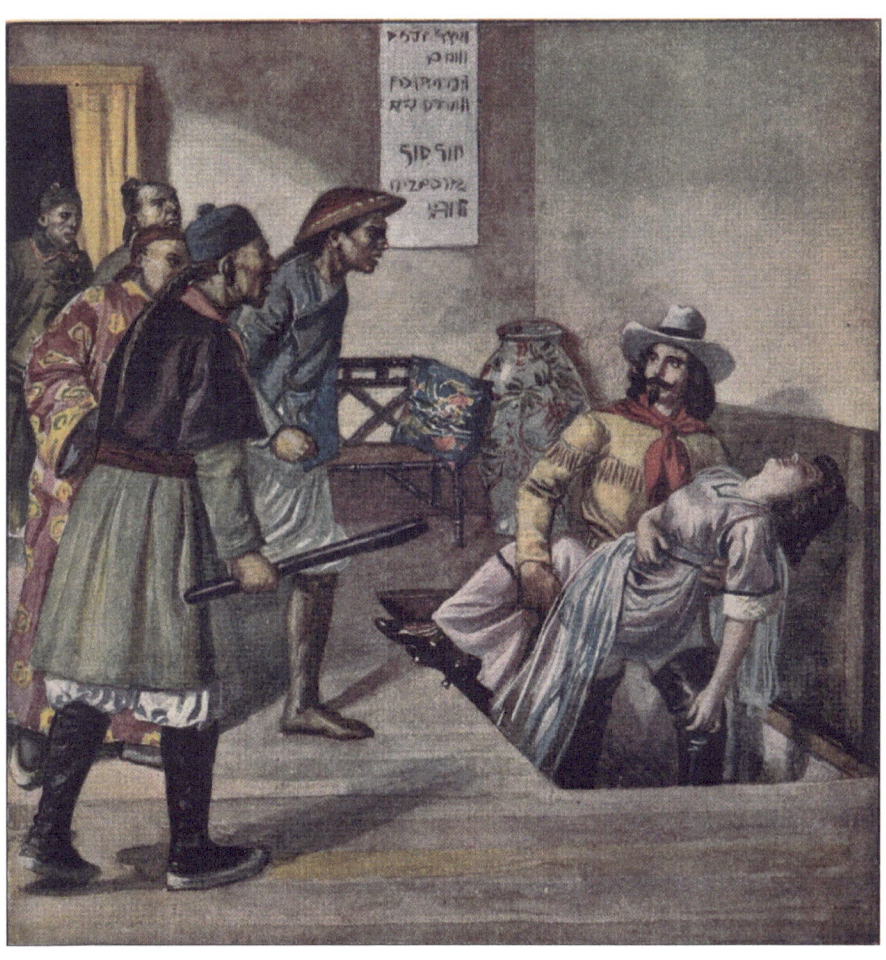

Claude Duval ou Au temps des Puritains d'Angleterre (In the Time of the English Puritans) No. 43. Les Hommes Noir (The Black Men) by Charlton Lea and translated by B.H. Gausseron. Cover by Robert Prowse. Reprint of British *Claude Duval Library* No. <u>43, 1903.</u>

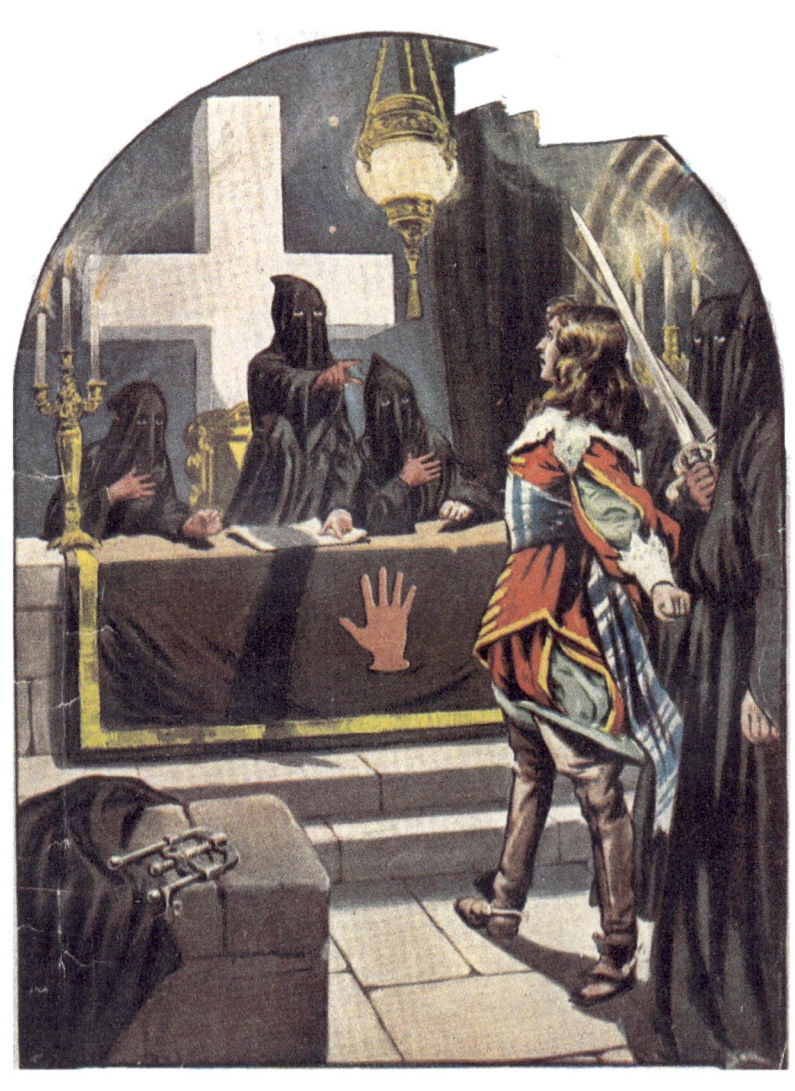

Tim & Tom Los pequños Robinsones (The Little Robinsons) No. 8, circa 1930. El Loco de la Isla (The Crazy Man of the Island). Anonymous (by Eleme), art by Toullot.

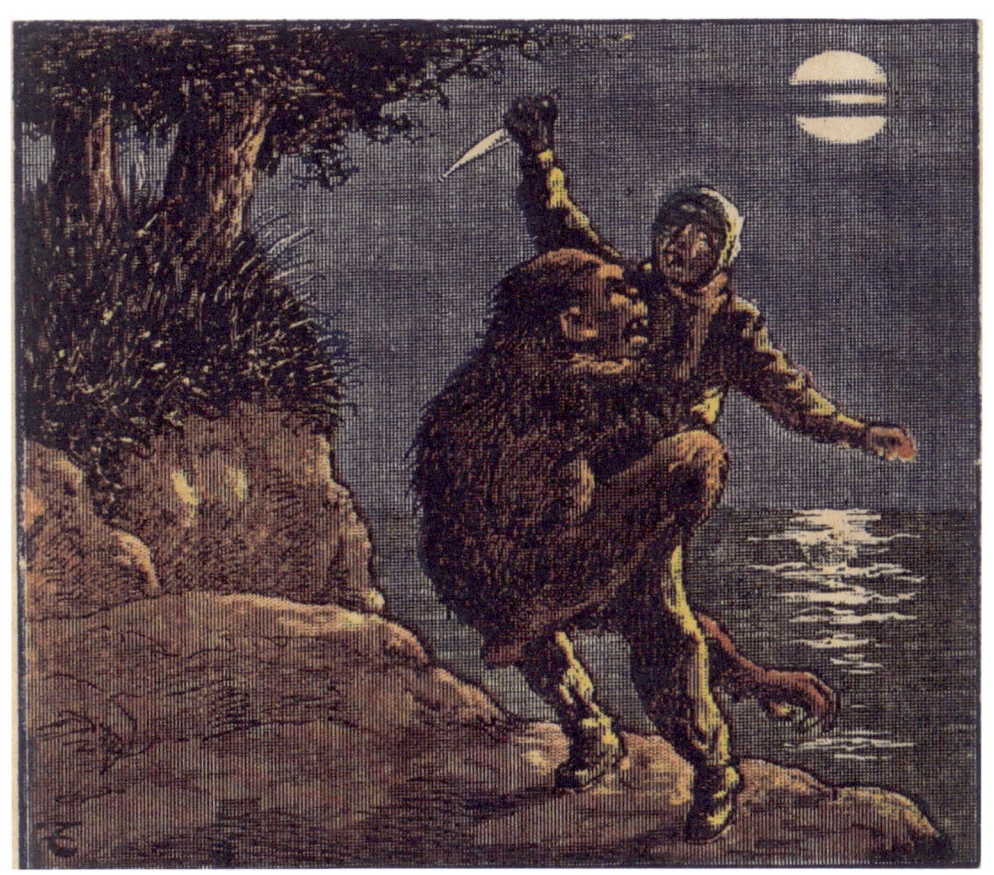

Aventuras Extraordinarias La Vuelta al Mundo por un Pillete Yanqui y su Perro (Extraordinary Adventures The Trip around the World of a Yankee Scamp and his Dog) No. 3,1920s. Terribles Peripecias de Tom (Tom's Terrible Adventures) by Rafael Nogueras Oller.

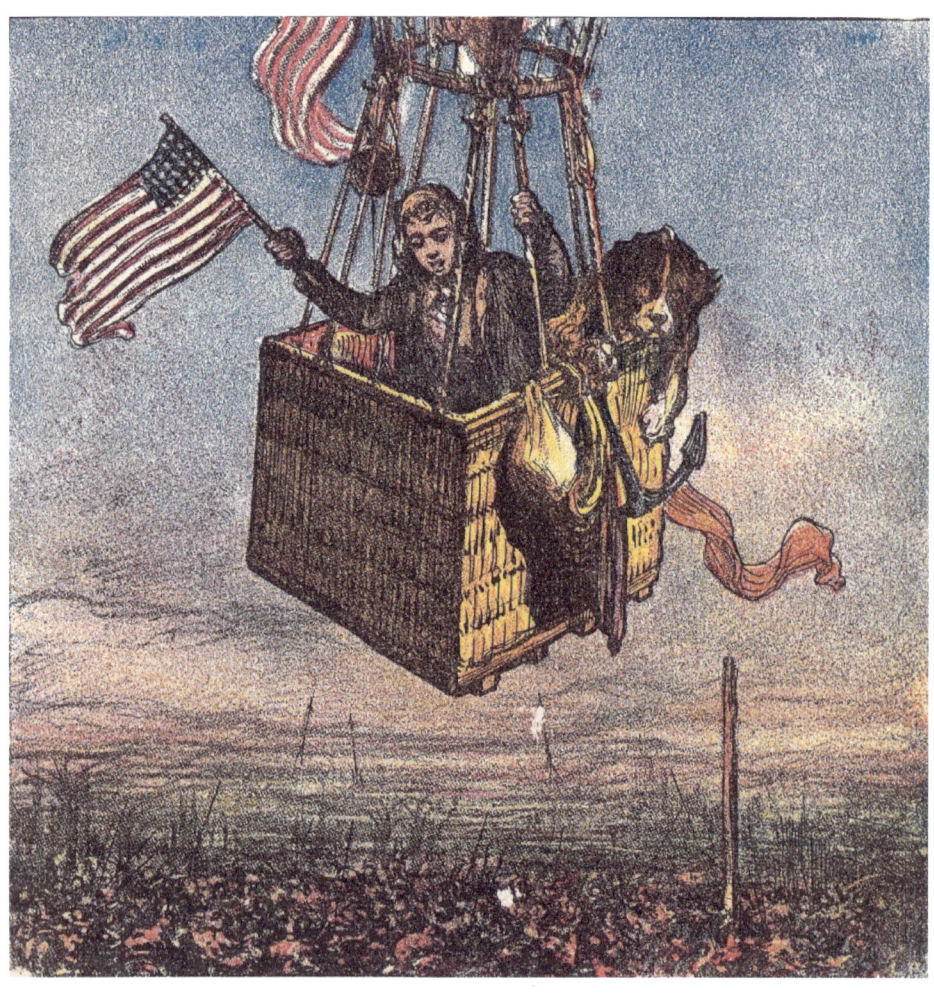

Ultimos Episodios de Nick Carter No. 91, circa 1920.
El Circo Embrujado (The Haunted Circus), anony-
mous, reprint with new cover by Luis Palao of *New
Nick Carter Weekly* No. 636, March 6, 1909.

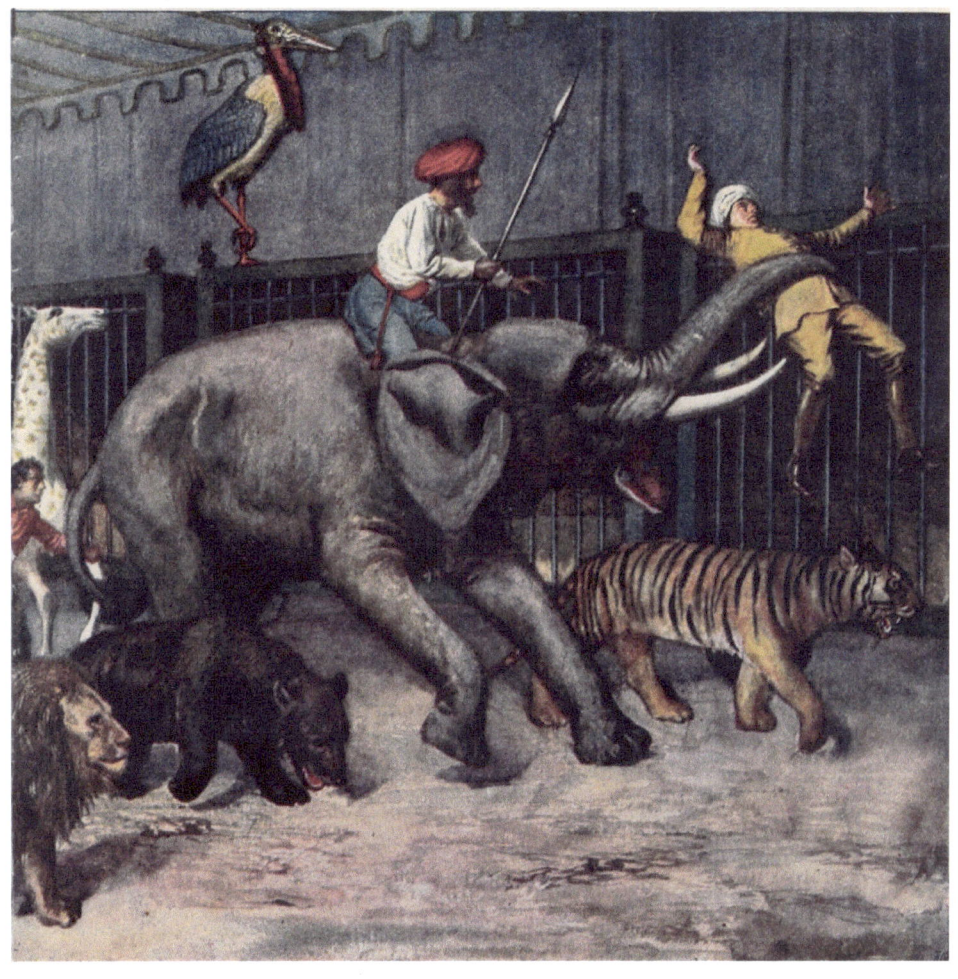

Buffalo-Bill L'Eroe del Wild West (Hero of the...) No. 118, 1929. I mostri della foresta (Forest Monsters), anonymous, cover by T. Scarpelli (signed).

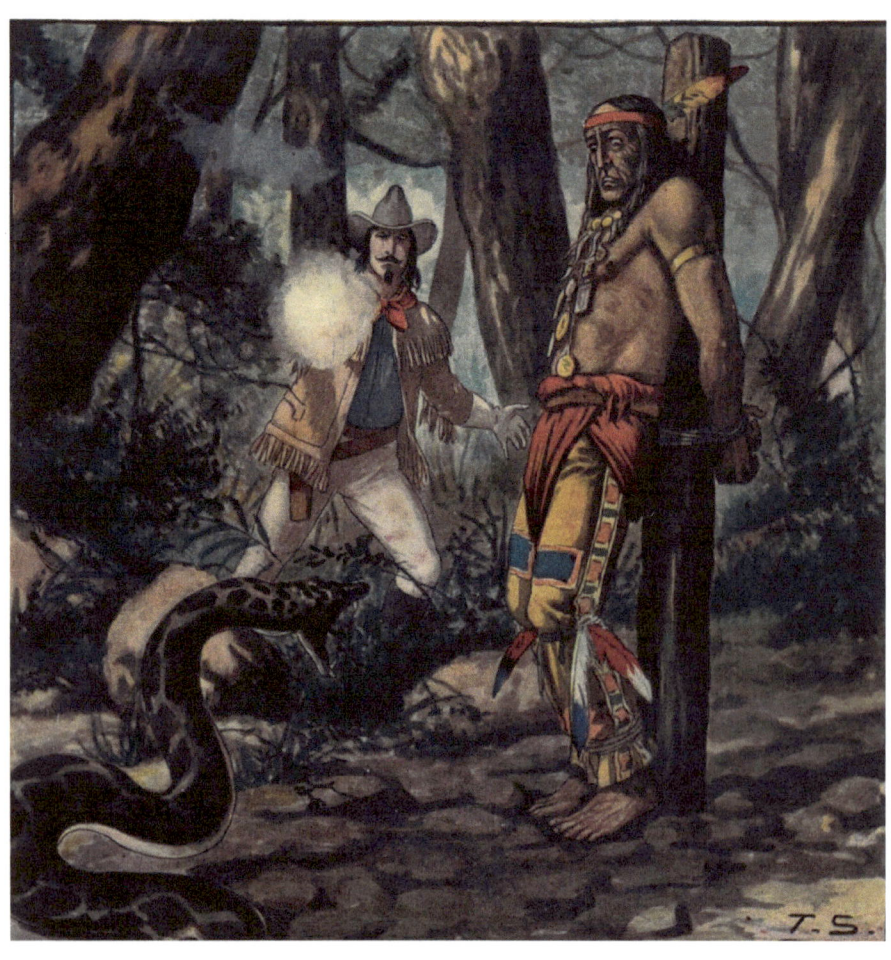

Texas Jack No. 22, 1906, Die schwarze Hand von Texas (The Black Hand of Texas), anonymous.

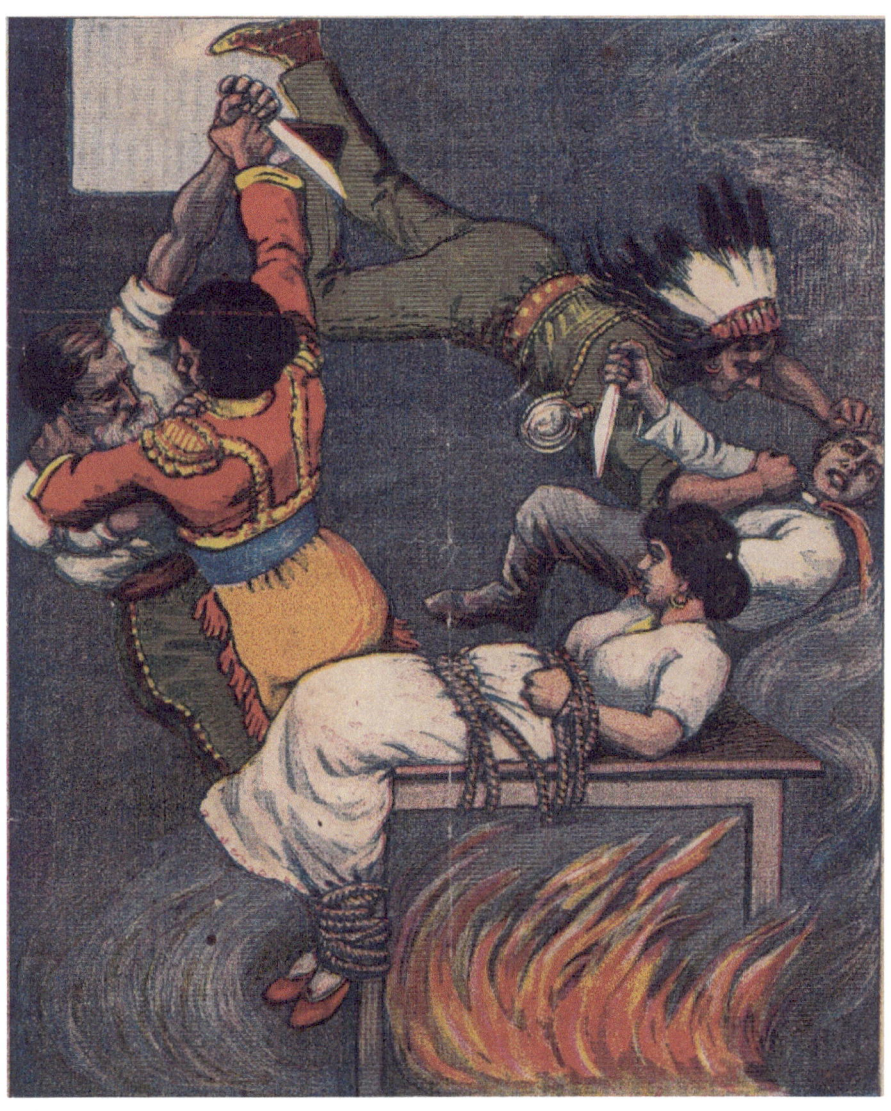

Cortacabezas el Explorador Invencible (Headchopper the Invincible Explorer) No. 10, circa 1930. El gigante solitario (The Lonely Giant), anonymous, cover by Niel (Daniel Masgoumiery i Pena), signed.

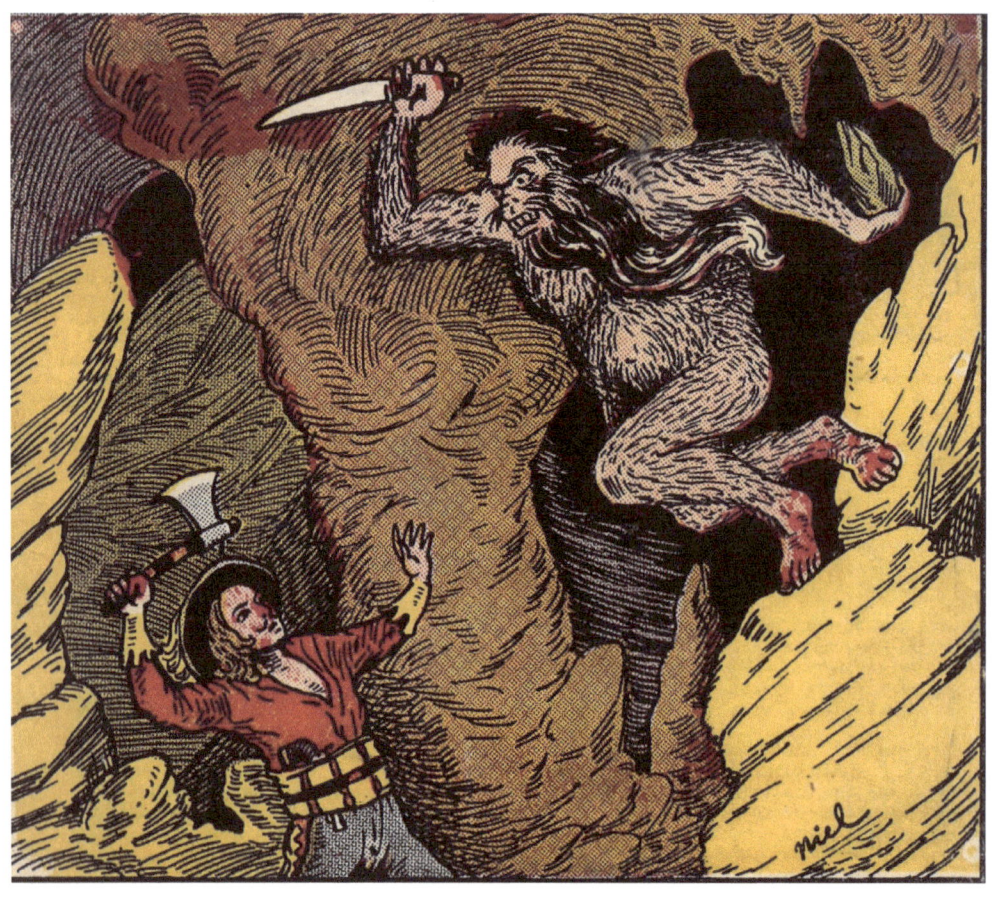

Tex, el Rey de las Pistolas (King of the Pistols) No. 3, circa 1933. La sombra de la horca (The Shadow of the Gallows).

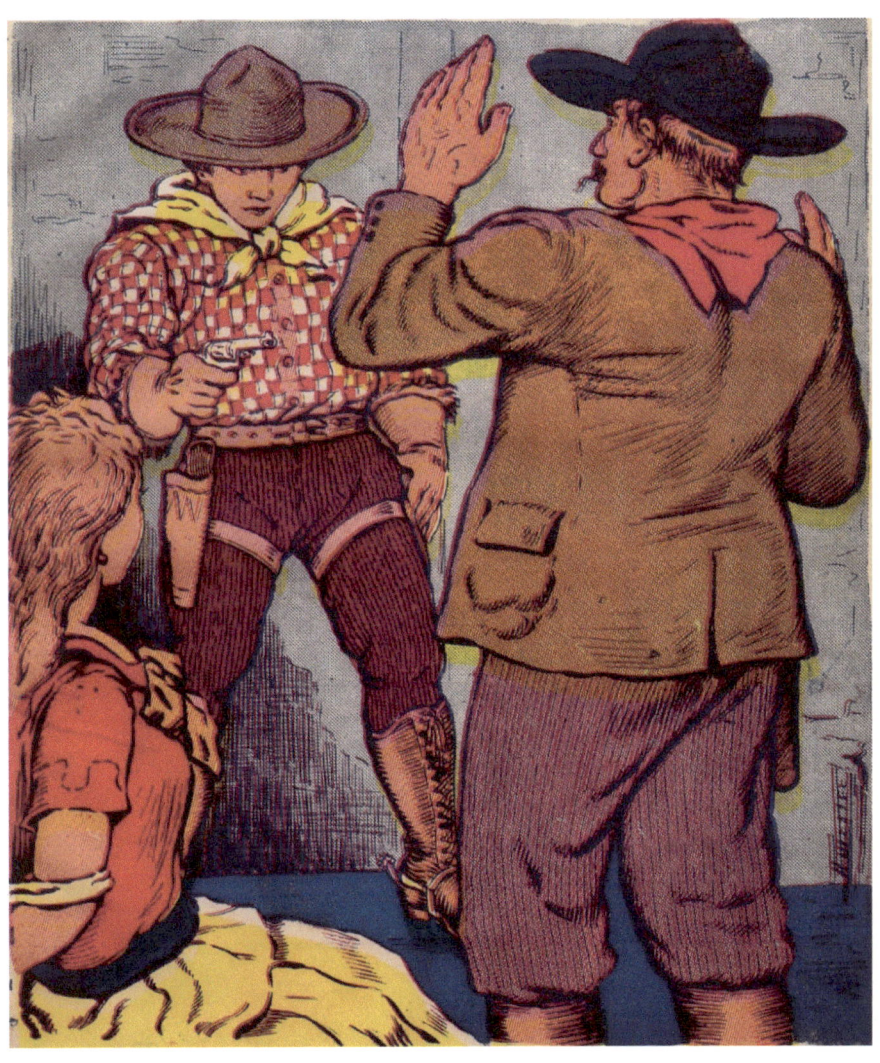

Ultimos Episodios de Nick Carter No. 75, 1920s.
Tragedia Aerea (Aerial Tragedy), anonymous, cover
by Luis Palao.

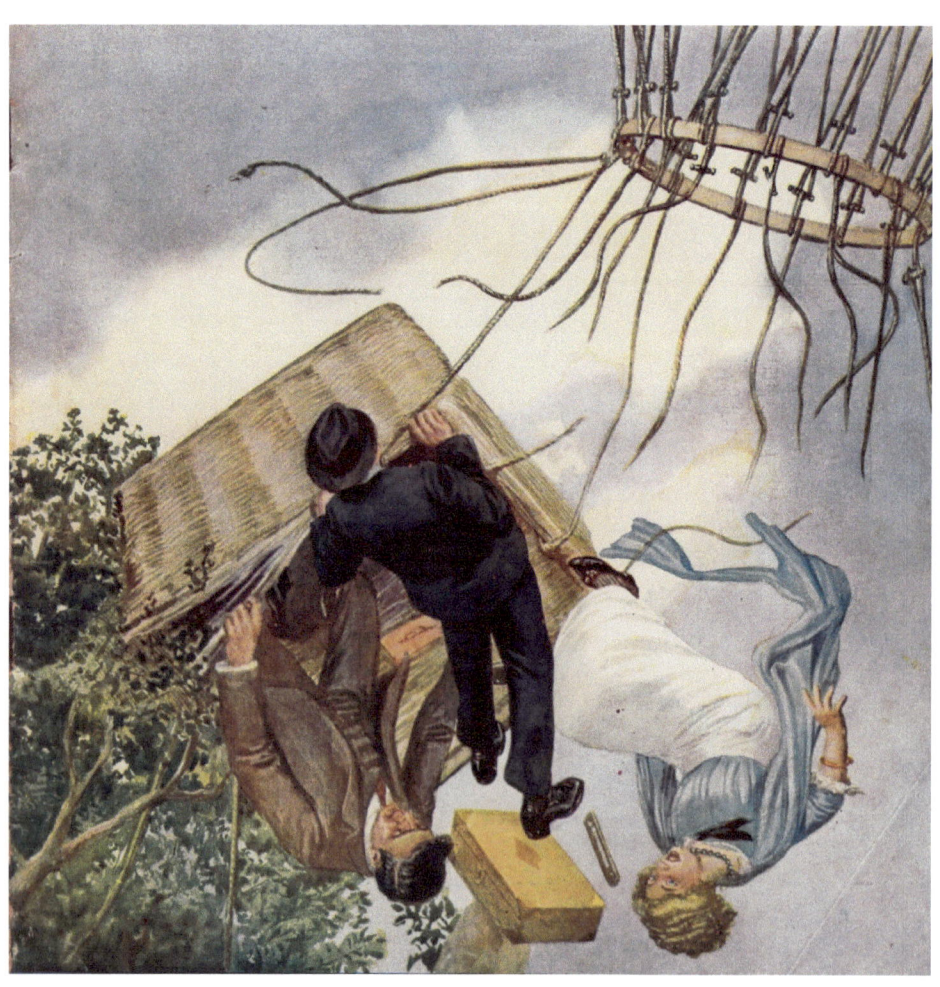

Lord Lister, Conocido por Raffles el Rey de los Ladrones (Lord Lister, Known as Raffles, King of Thieves) No. 4, circa 1910. El Tesoro de; un sarcótago (A Coffin's Treasure), anonymous (Kurt Matull and Theo Blanensee). Spanish reprint of German *Lord Lister* No. 4, 1908).

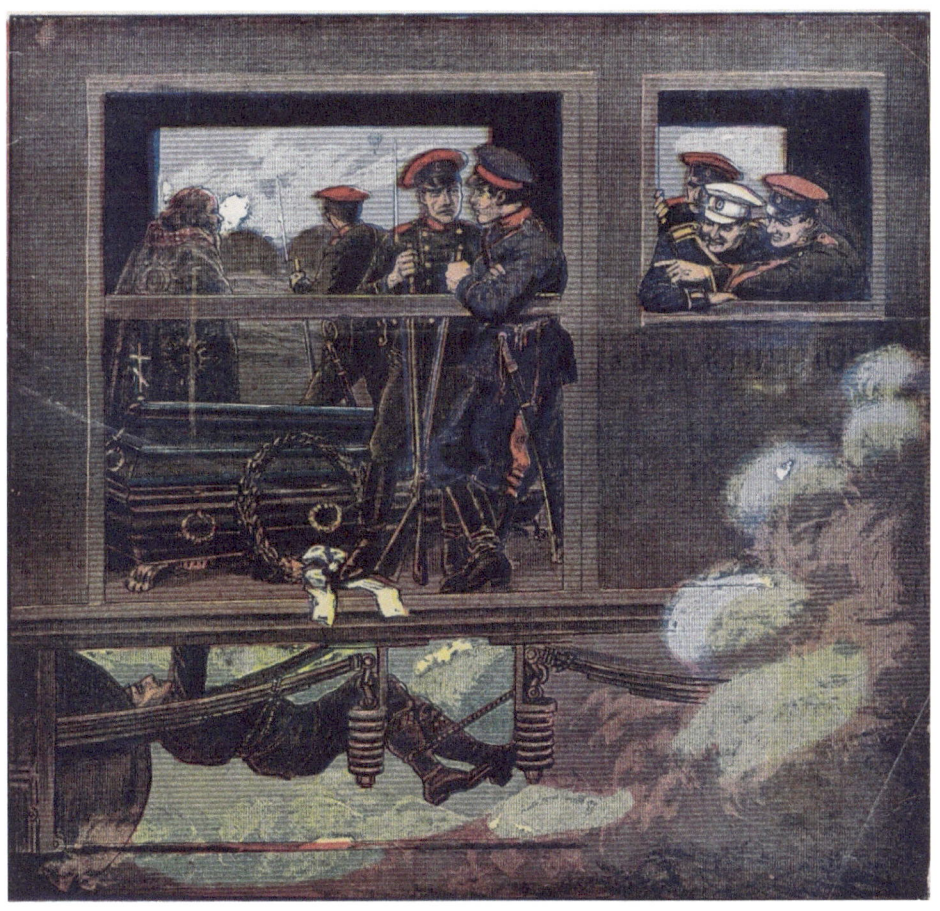

Les Merveilleux Exploits de Buffalo-Bill (Buffalo Bill's Wonderful Adventures) No. 14, 1946. Les compagnons de la croix fulgurante (Companions of the Burning Corss) by George Fonval, art by Réne Brantonne, from Editiona Duclos, Paris. New story.

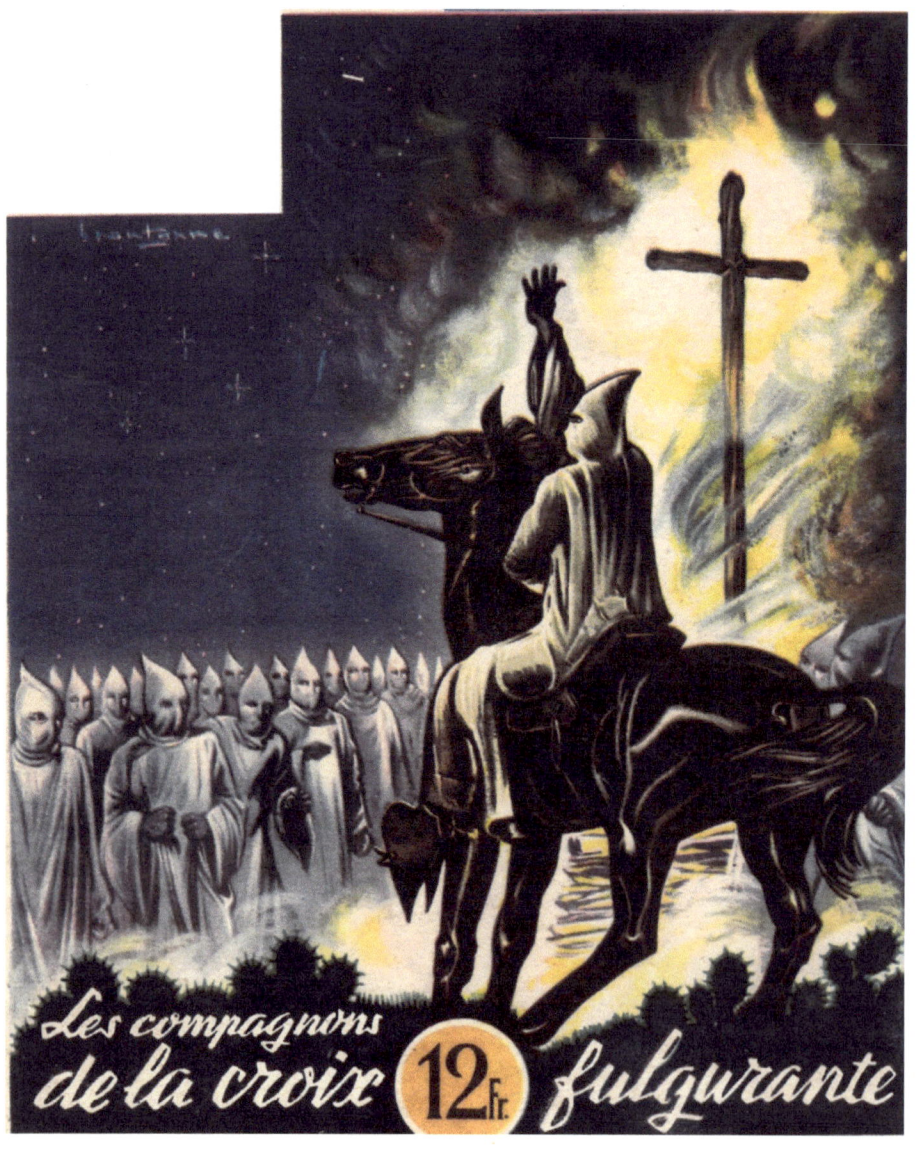

Buffalo-Bill l'eroe del Wild West No. 36, (1947. I rapitori di ragazze (The Child Abductors), anonymous, cover by T. Scarpelli (signed).

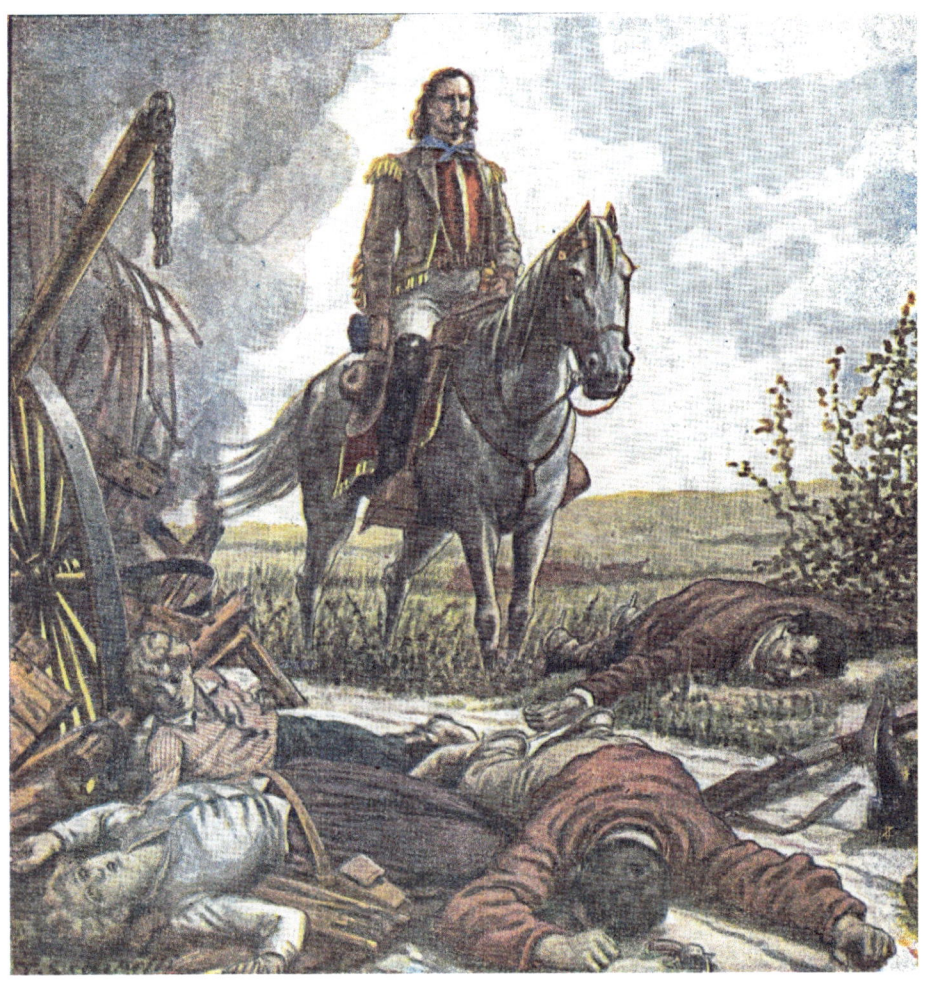

Jim Brade el Ciclón Tejano (Jim Brady the Texas Twister) No. 17, cicrca 1930. La Noche Sangrienta de San Francisco (The Bloody Night in San Francisco), anonymous.

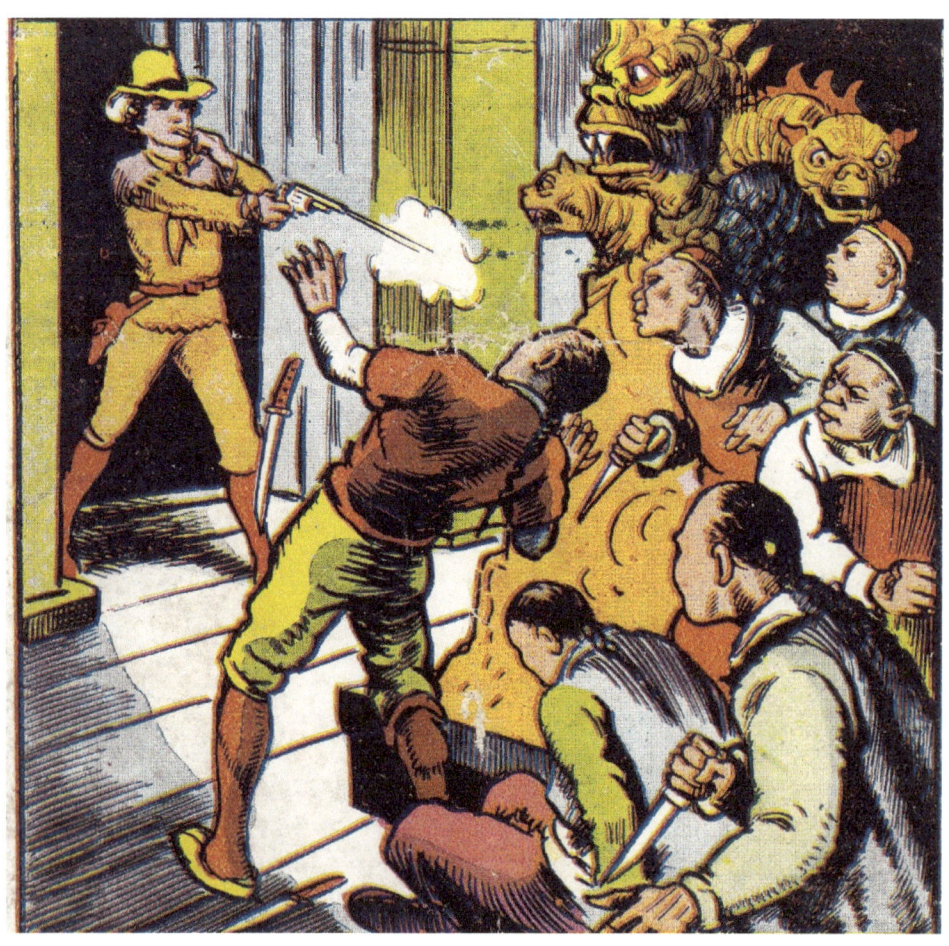

La Vuelta al Mundo de dos Pilletes (Two Scamps Around the World) No. 29, 1920s. La sentencia de muerte (The Death Sentence) by El Conde Henri de la Vaulx and Anrould Galopin, cover by Luis Palao.

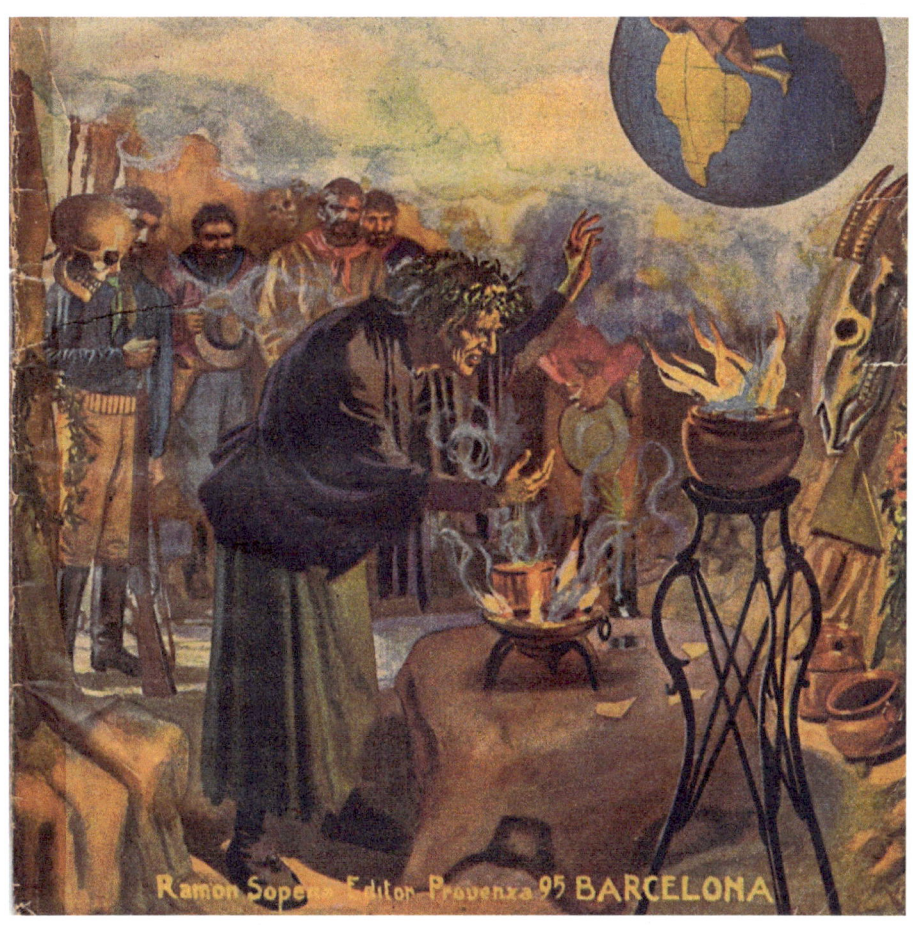

Pieles Rojas Contra Blancos (Red Skins versus Whites) No. 8, 1915. Los Antepasados del Jefe de los Mohicanos (The Mohican Chief's Forefathers), anonymous. Reprint of French dime novel *Les Chefs Indiens Célèbres* No. 8, 1909.

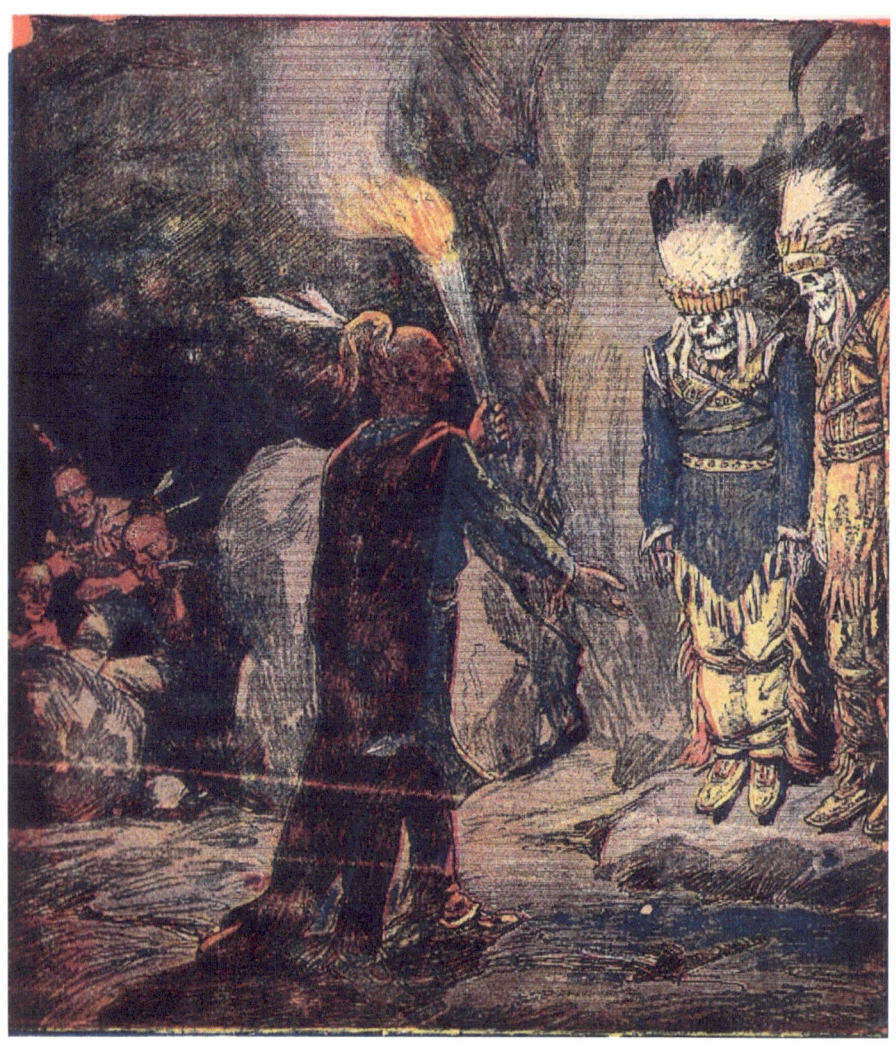

Mack-Wan el Invencible No. 2, 1933. Los Niños Mutilados (The Mutilated Children), anonymous (José Canellas Casals), cover by Marc Farell.

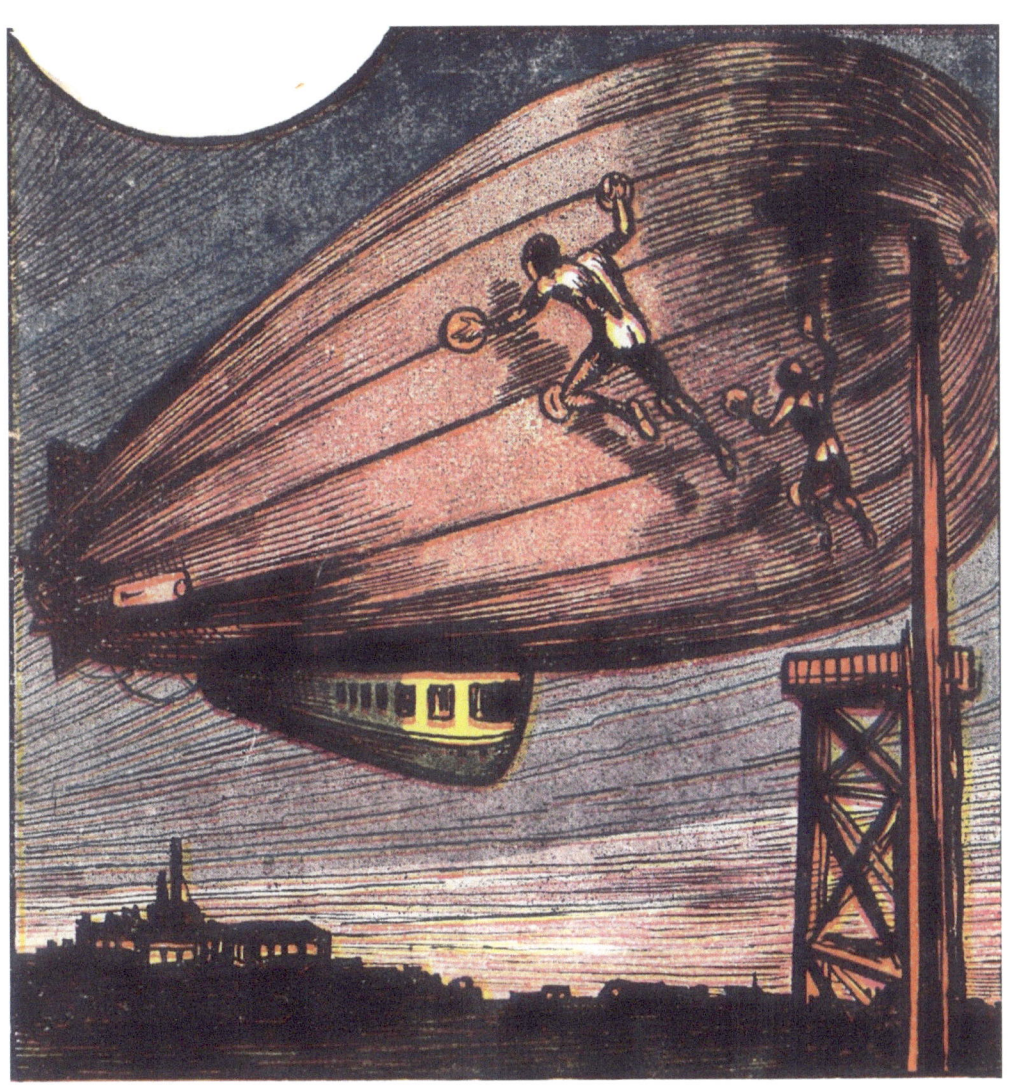

El Folletin No. Extraordinario, 1926. La Dama de las Camelias (The Lady of the Camellias) by Alejando Dumas (first printed in 1848), cover by Oscar.

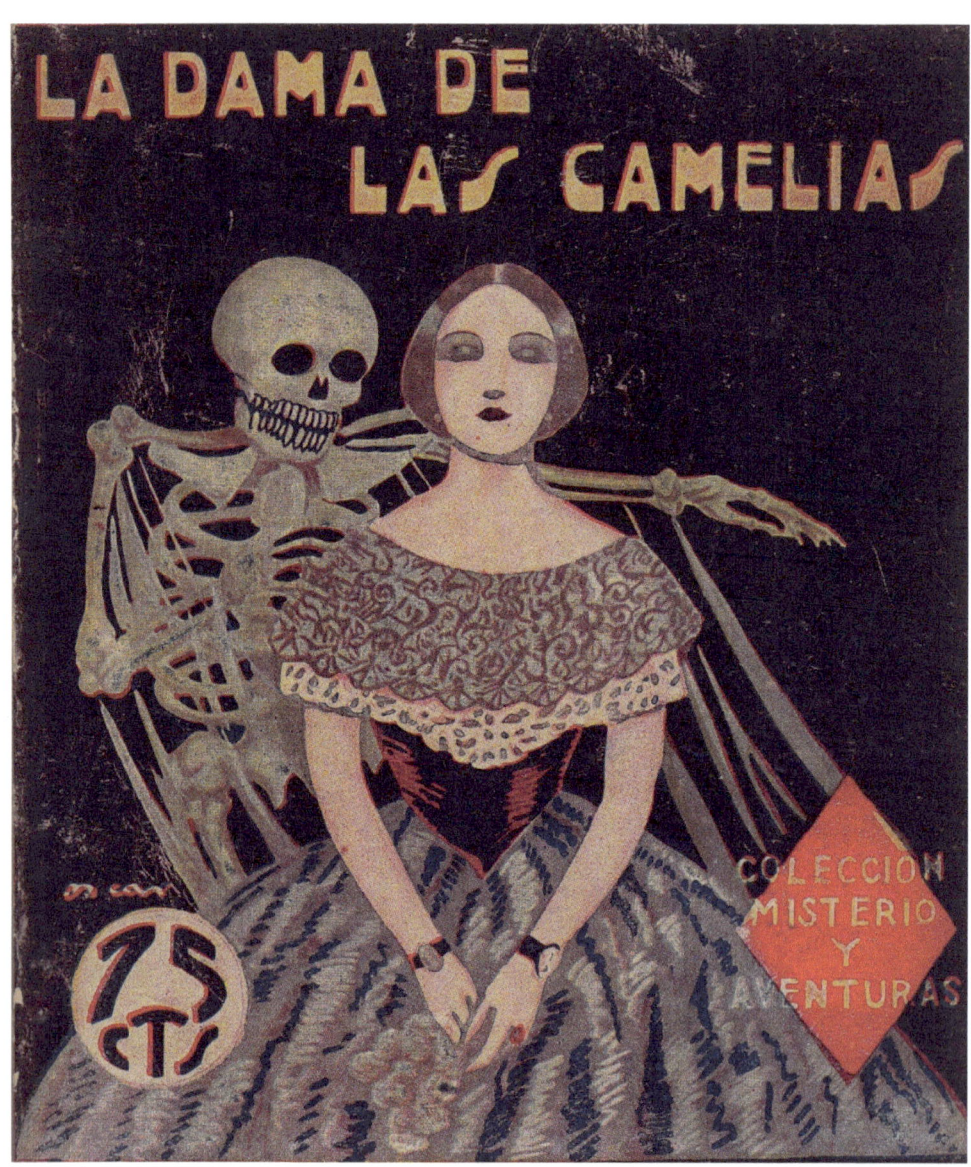

Ultimos Episodios de Nick Carter No. 44, circa 1920. El Fantasma de Fuego (The Ghost of Fire), anonymous (probably Frederick Van Rensselaer Dey), cover by Luis Palao. Spanish reprint with new cover of *Nick Carter Weekly* No. 555, August 17, 1907.

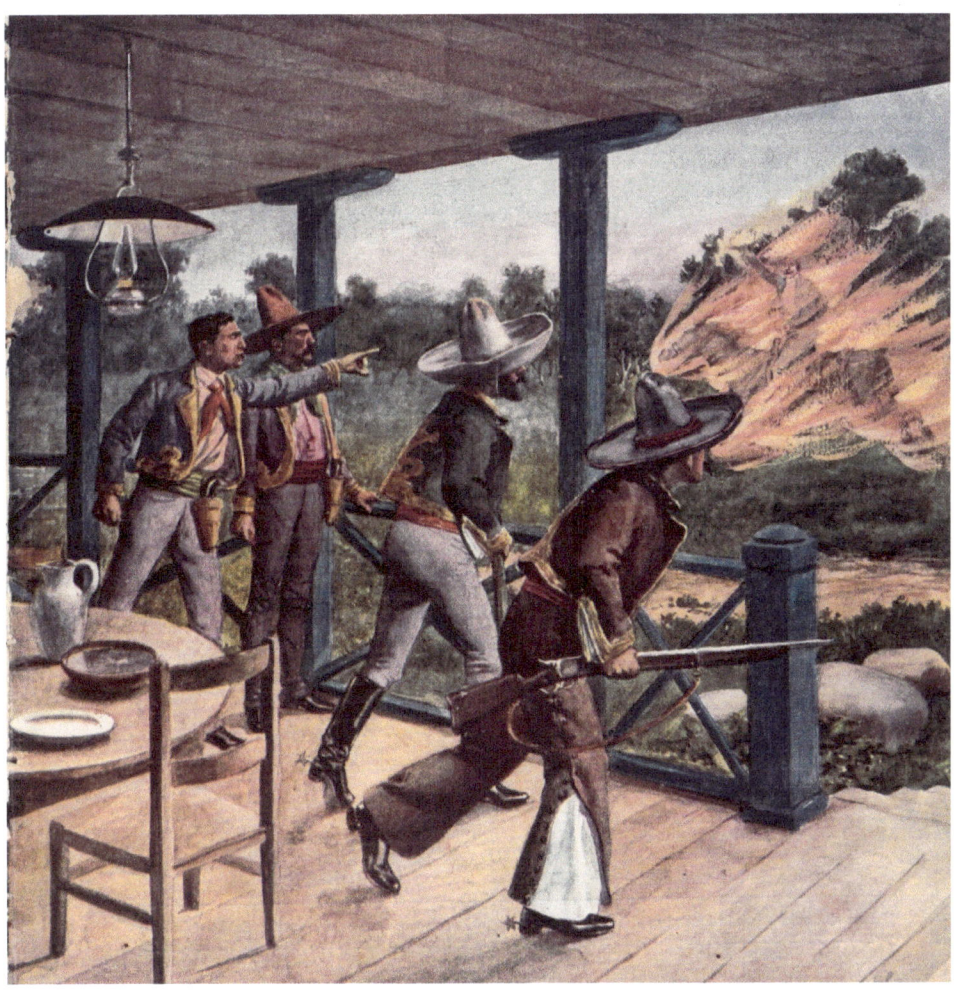

Prinzessin Übermut (The Fresh Princess, or Princess Audacious, Princess Arrogance, etc.) No. 345, circa 1918. Eine Serie lustiger Backfischstreiche (A series of funny schoolgirl pranks), Die Geisterruine (Spirits of the Ruins or Ruinous Spirits or Poltergiest).

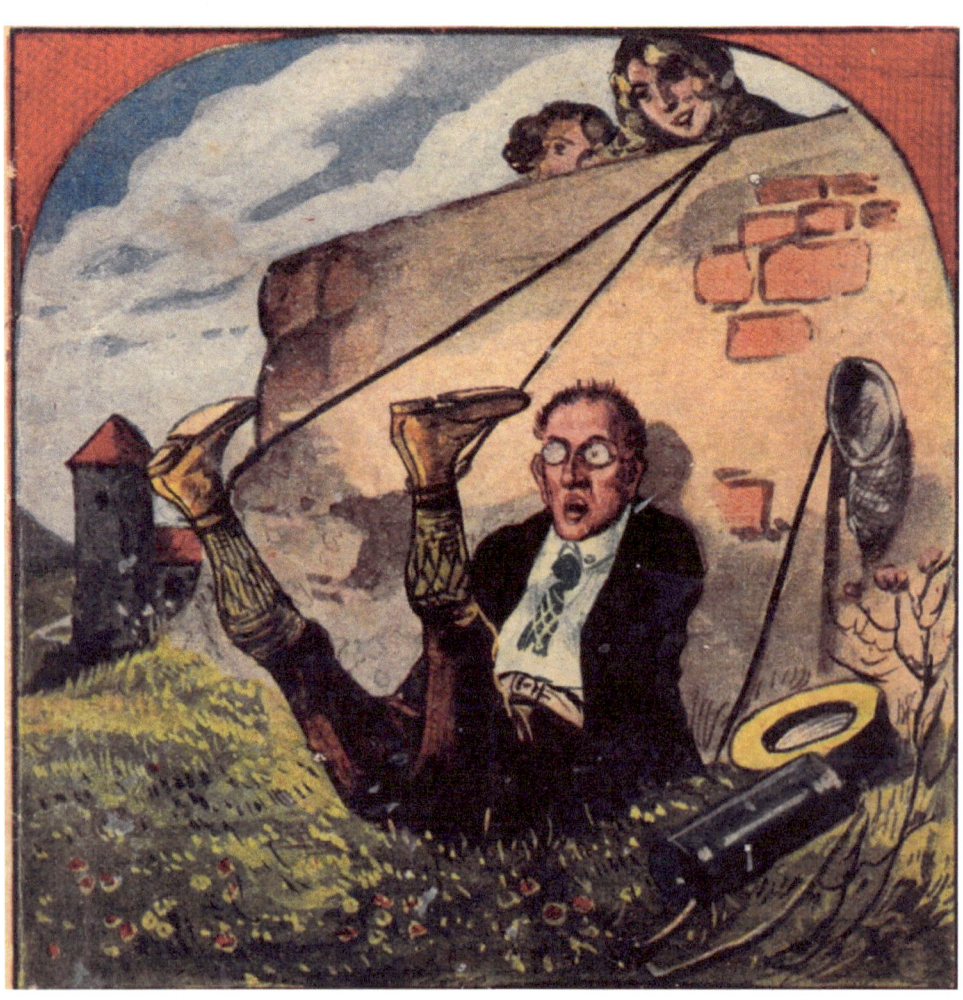

Sitting Bull El Ultimo Piel Roja (The last Redskin) No. 8, early 1930s. La Tumba de las Luces Rojas (The Grave of Red Lights), anonymous.

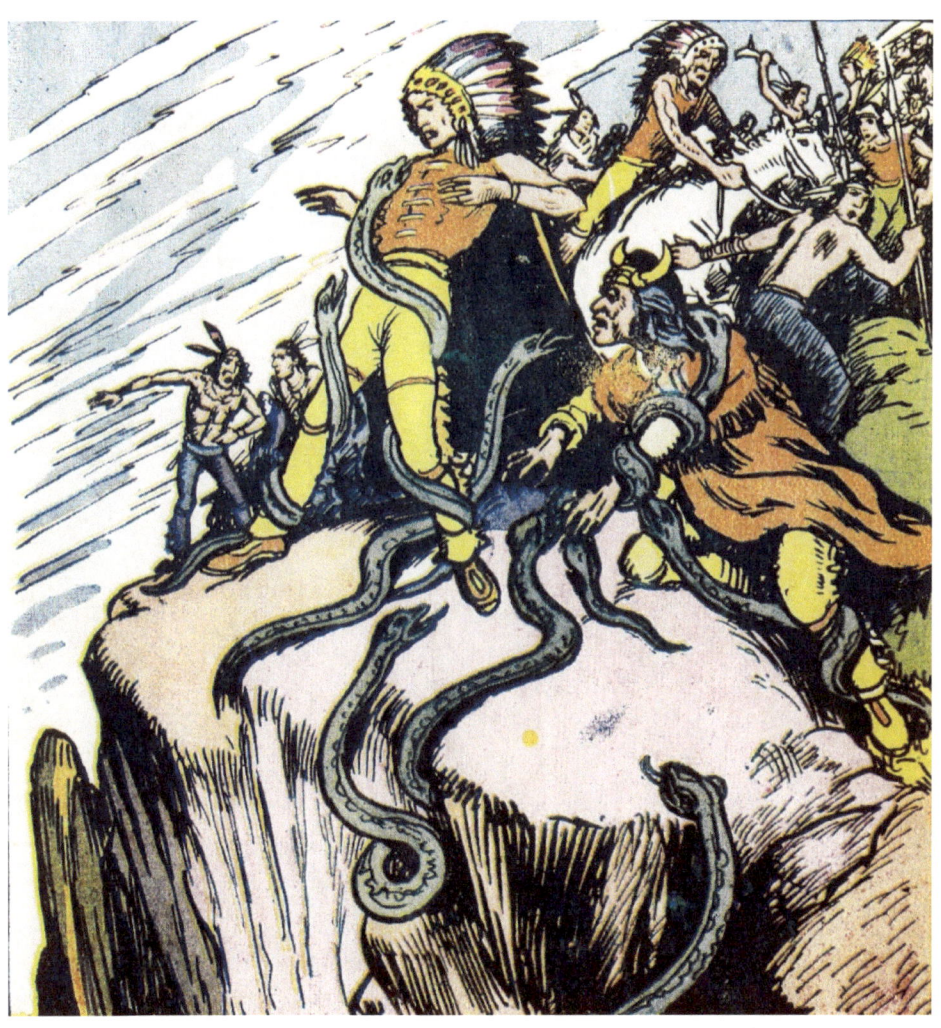

Voltereta el Muchacho de Goma (Somersault the Rubber Boy) No. 1, circa 1920. Aventuras de un Niño Robado (Adventures of a Kidnapped Child), anonymous, art by Boix.

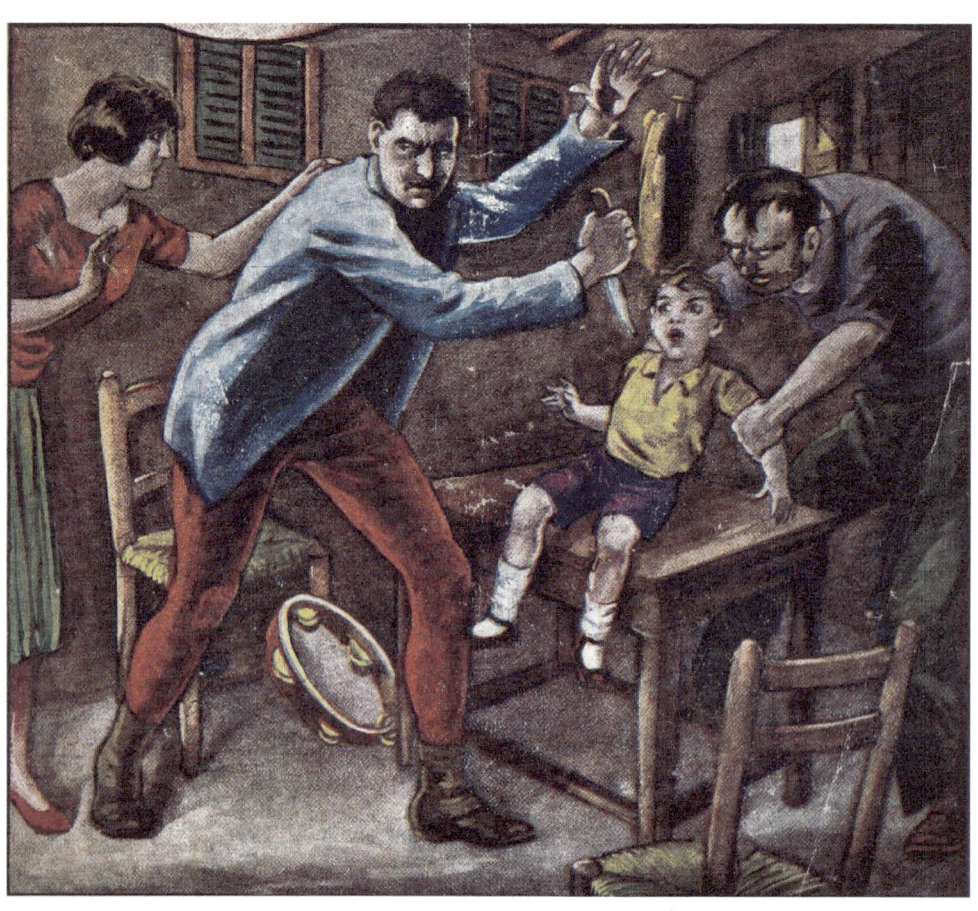

Ultimos Episodios de Nick Carter No. 80, circa 1920. Nick Carter Enterrado Vivo (Buried Alive), anonymous but probably Frederick Van Rensselaer Dey, new cover by Luis Palao. Reprinted from *New Nick Carter Weekly* No. 619, November 7, 1908, Down to The Grave, Or, Nick Carter Buried Alive. Reprinted again in *New Magnet Library* No. 1256, A War of Brains, Or, Nick Carter Buried Alive.

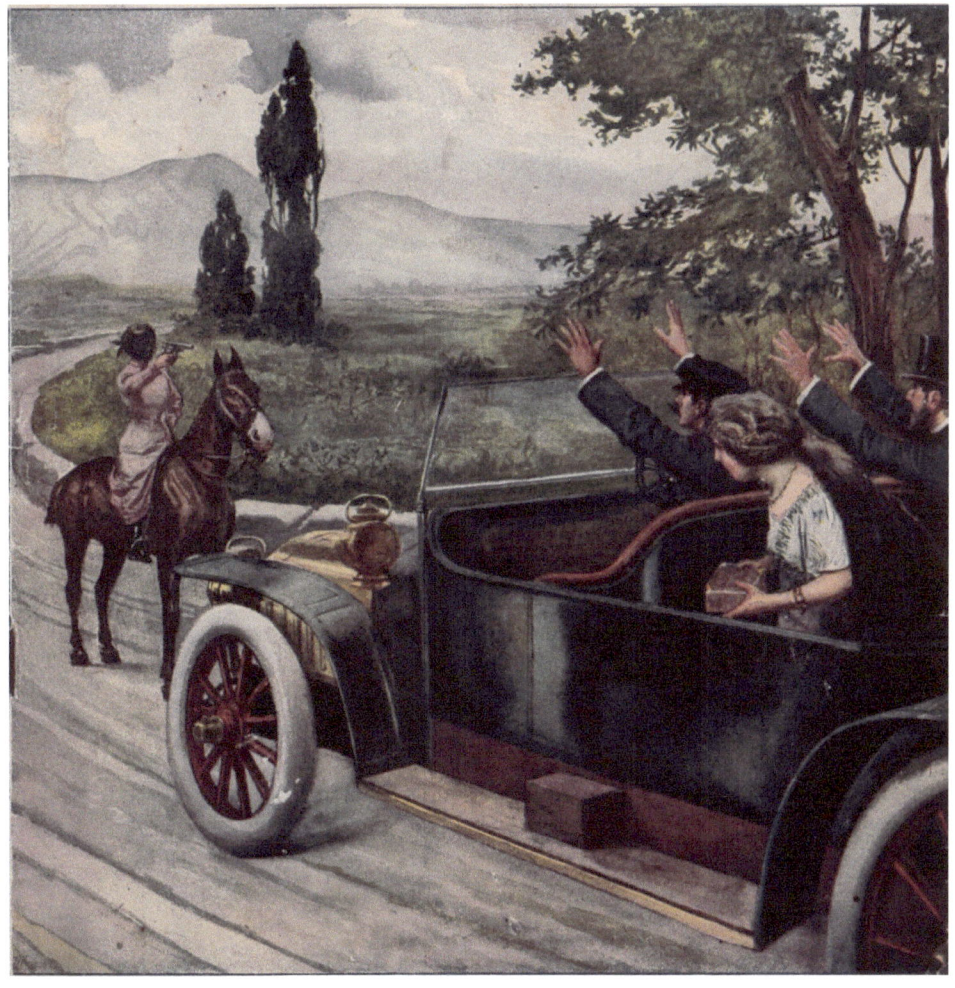

Texas Jack Der beühmteste Indianerkämpfer (Texas Jack the Famous Indian Fighter) No. 95, 1907. Die Femrichter des Ku-Klux-Clan (The Ku Klux Klan's Kangaroo Court), anonymous.

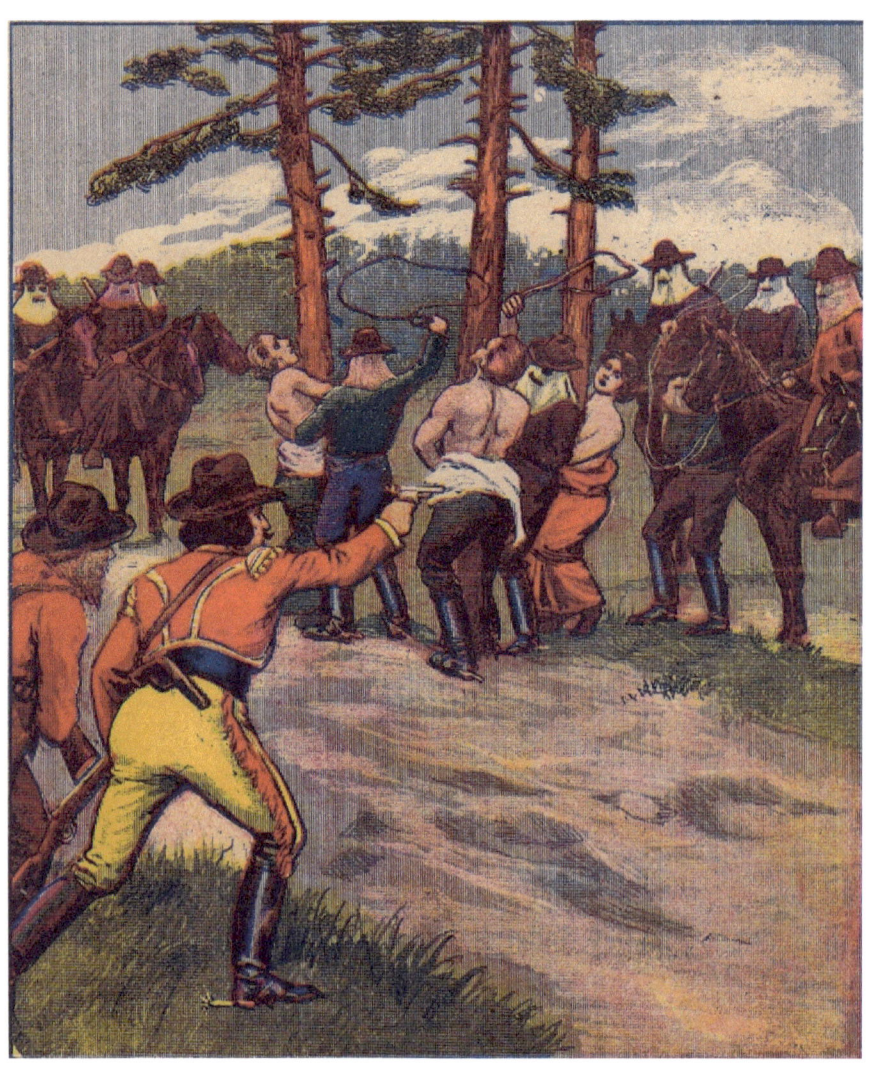

Nat Pinkerton der König der Detectivs (Nat Pinkerton, King of Detectives) No. 11, 1907. Der verbrecheriste Polizeichef (The Fake Police Chief, anonymous.

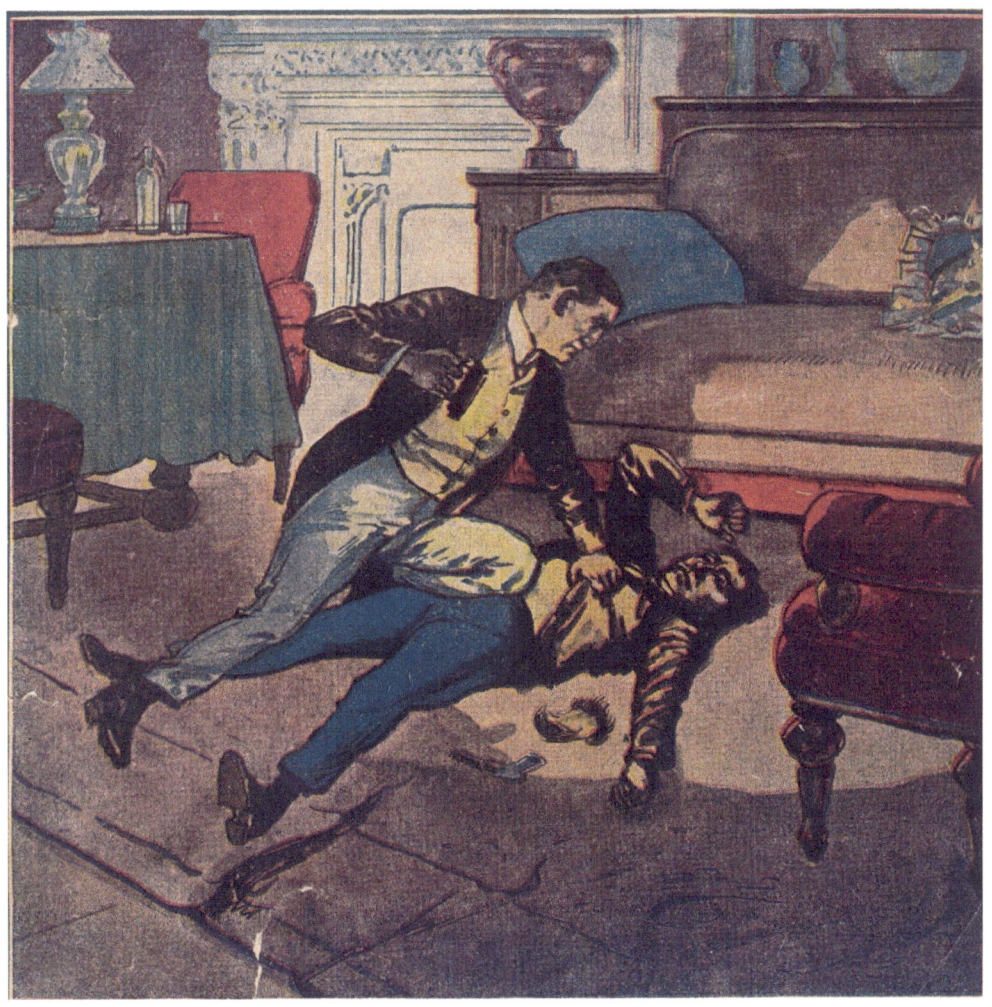

Sherlock Holmes Memorias intimas del rey de los detectives (Personal Memoirs of the King of Detectives) No. 7, 1934. En la Tumba junto a la maquina infernal (In the Tomb together with the Infernal Machine), anonymous (Theo Blanensee), cover and art by E. Ferrando.

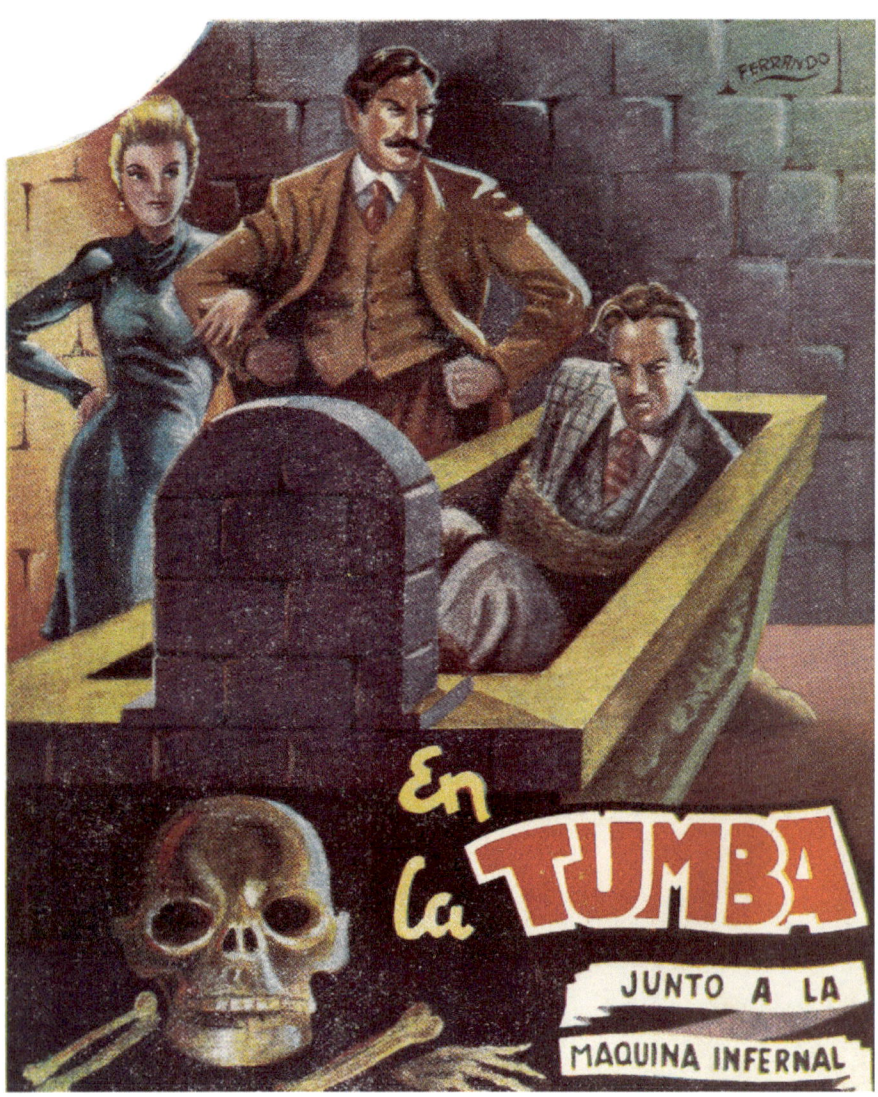

Tim Drake El héroe del Far-West No. 6, circa 1926. A las Puertas de la Muerte (At Death's Door).

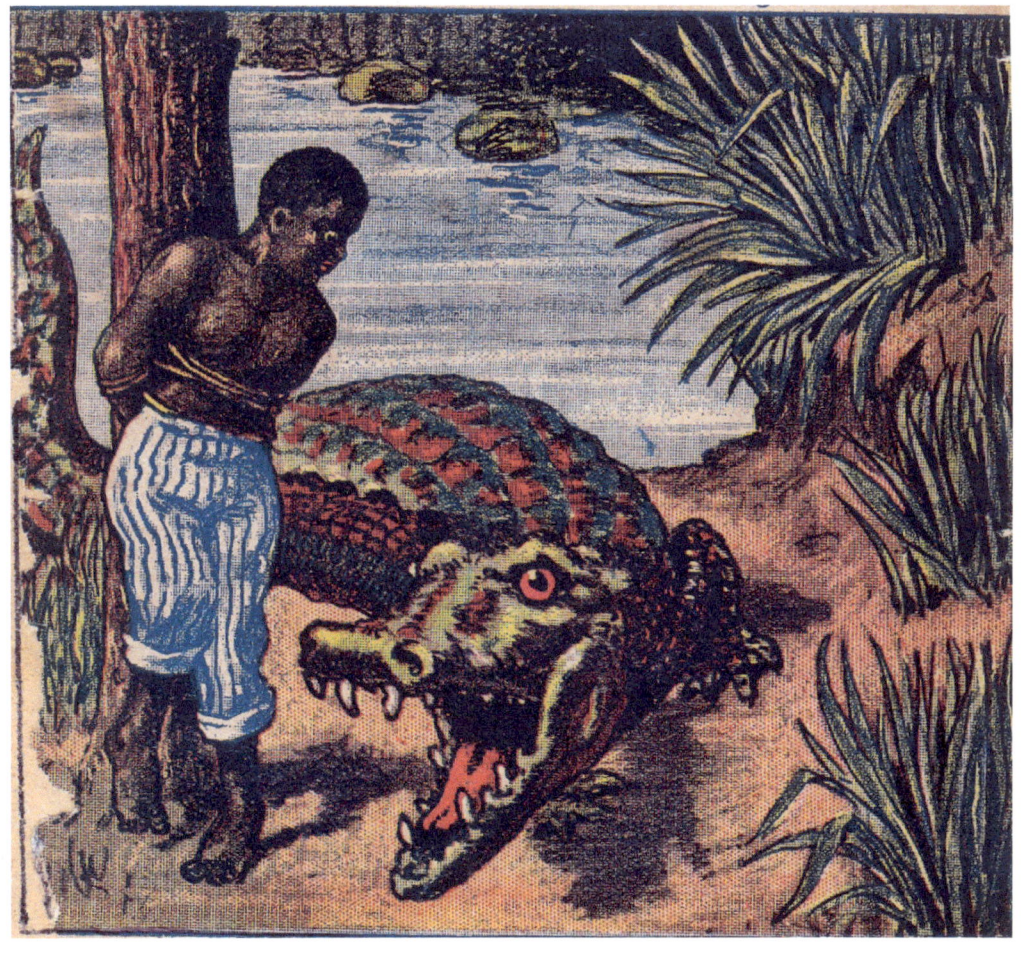

Nick Carter No. 163, March 19, 1933, The Mysterious Murderer of Falls River, anonymous. cover uncredited (T. Scarpelli?).

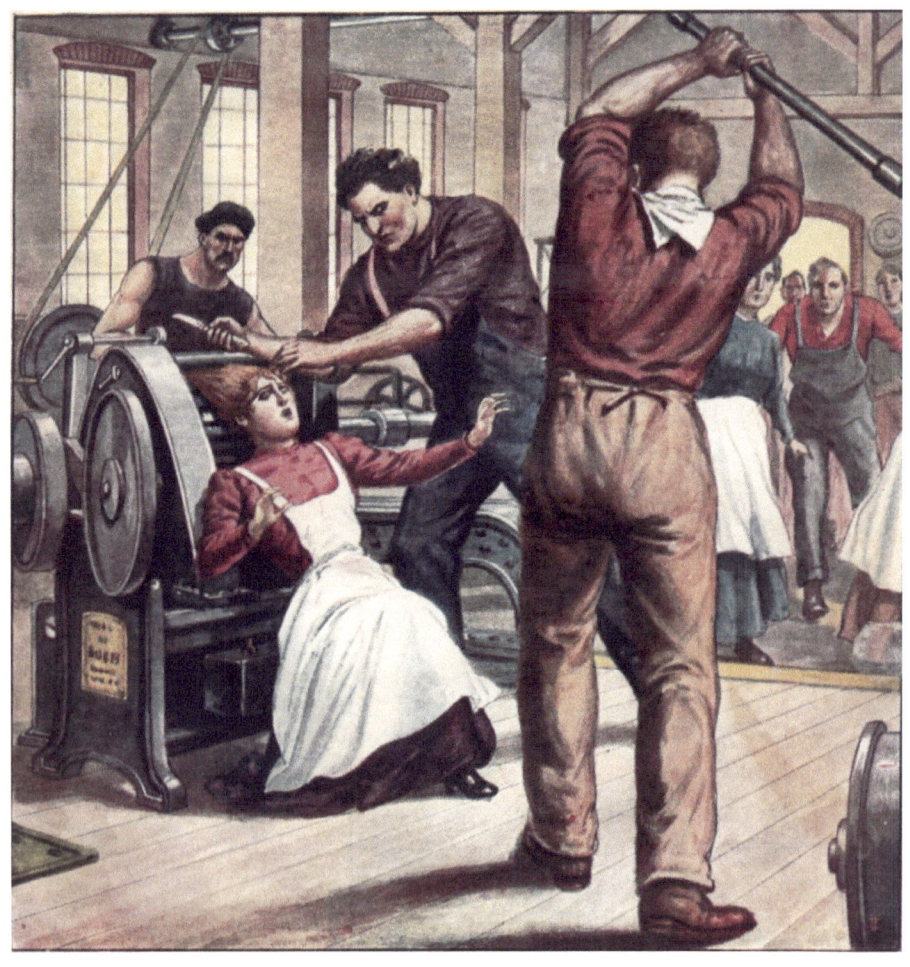

Jim Nay el Pequeño Aventurero No. 22, circa 1930.
En Siberia by Ernesto Pérez Donaz (signed).

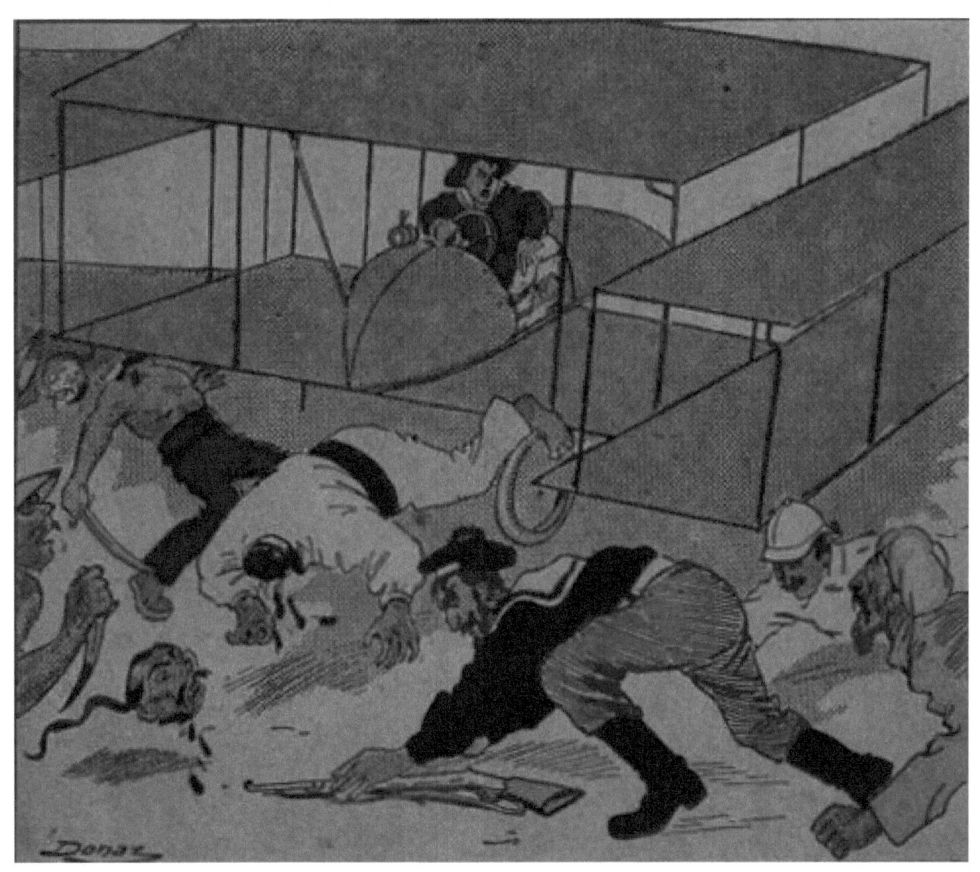

Los Maldicientes o Los Corozones de Cieno, novella de costumbres (The Slanderers; or, the Hearts of Silt, a Romance of Manners) No. 1, circa 1900. By Don Julian Castellanos y Velasco, published by Juan Muñoz Sánchez, Madrid.

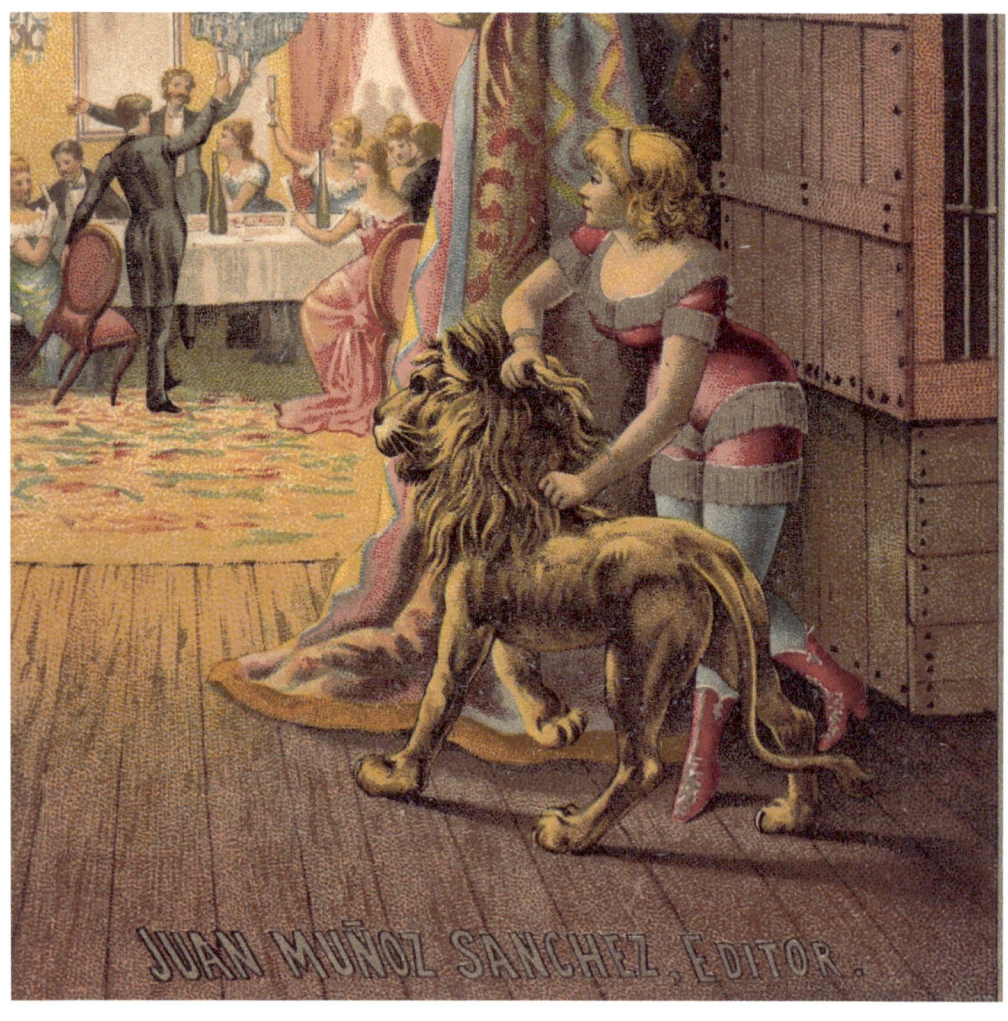

Buffalo-Bill l'eroe del Wild West No. 32, 1946.
Serpente Selvaggio, l'indiano Cheyenne (Wild Snake,
the Cheyenne Indian), anonymous, cover by T.
Scarpelli (signed).

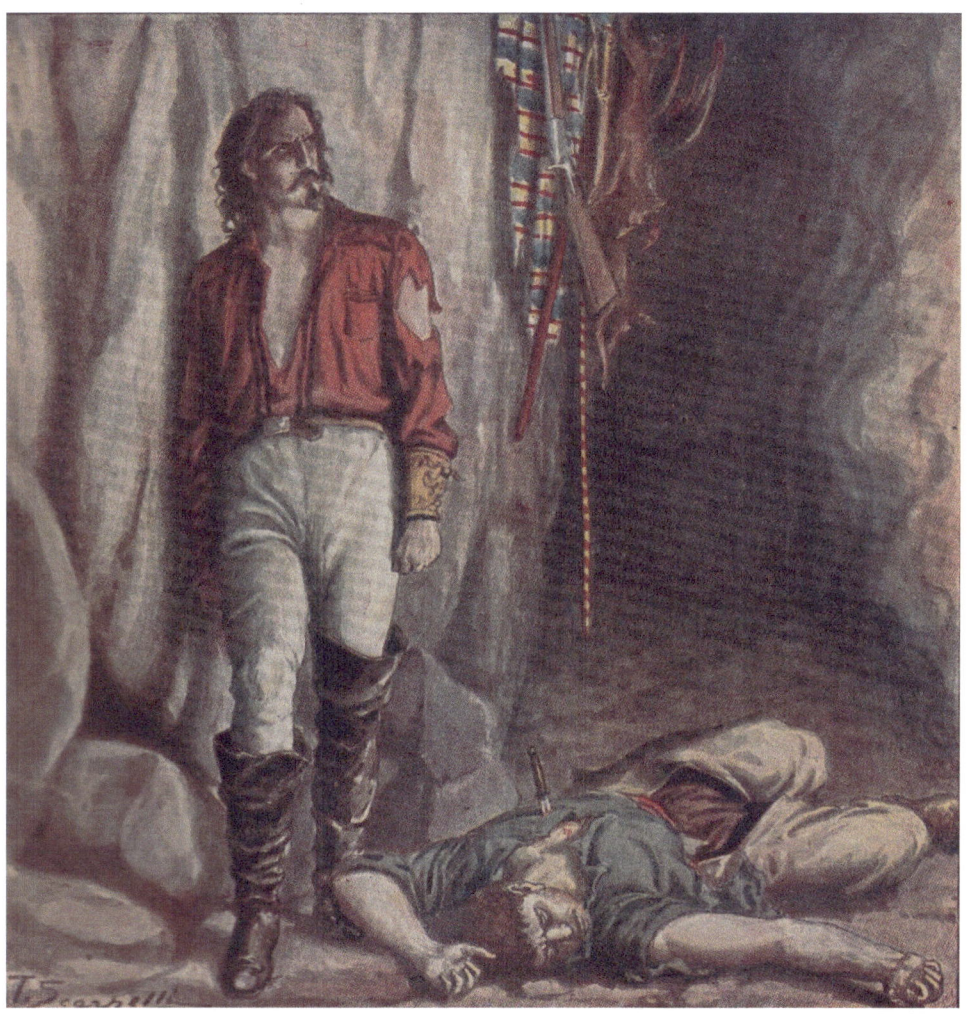

Cortacabezas de Explorador Invencible (Head-chopper, the Invincible Explorer) No. 12, 1930s. El puñal de los Nyam Nyam (The Dagger of the Nyam Nyam), anonymous, cover by Niel (Daniel Masgoumiery i Pena, 1879-1942). Niel was a plumber by profession, a leader of the Federal Council and editor of *North Wind and Future*, a workers' solidarity publication which advocated Catalan anarchism. He also published *Eppur si muove* (*And Yet It Moves*, 1906), a compendium of anarchist ideology.

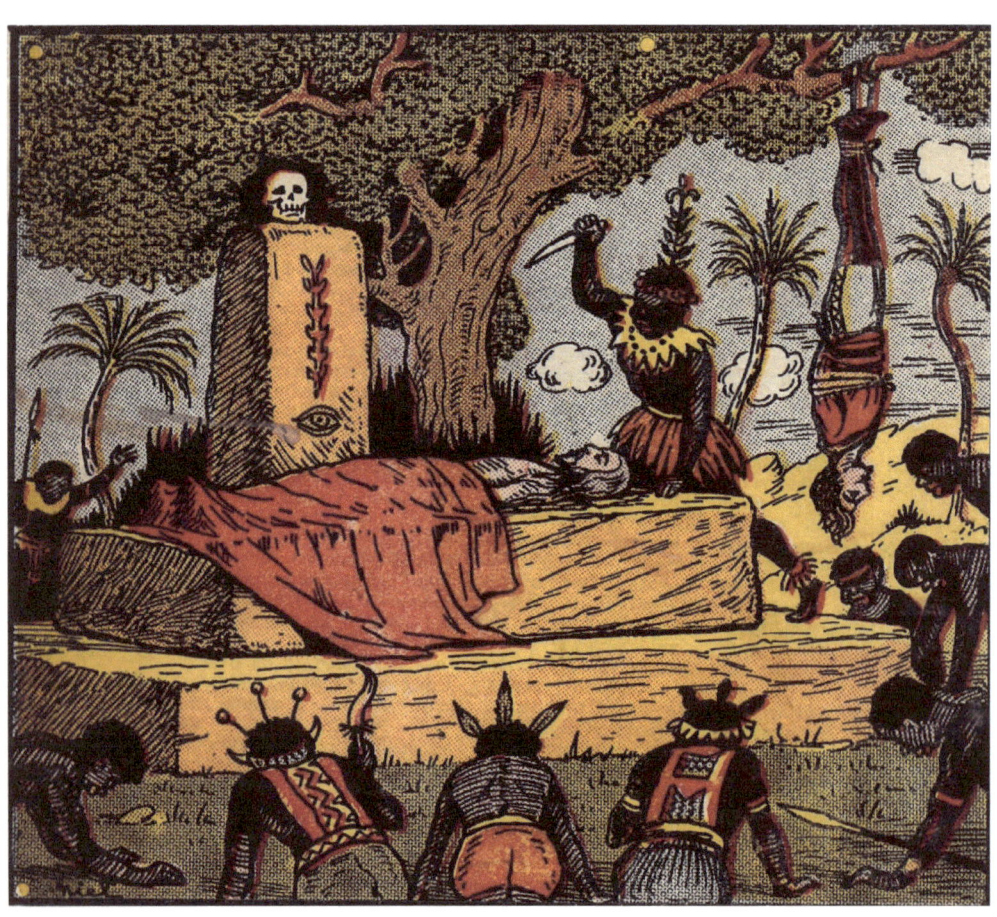

Dick Norton El Heroe del Far-West No. 66, circa 1930. El Espia Rojo (The Red Spy), anonymous.

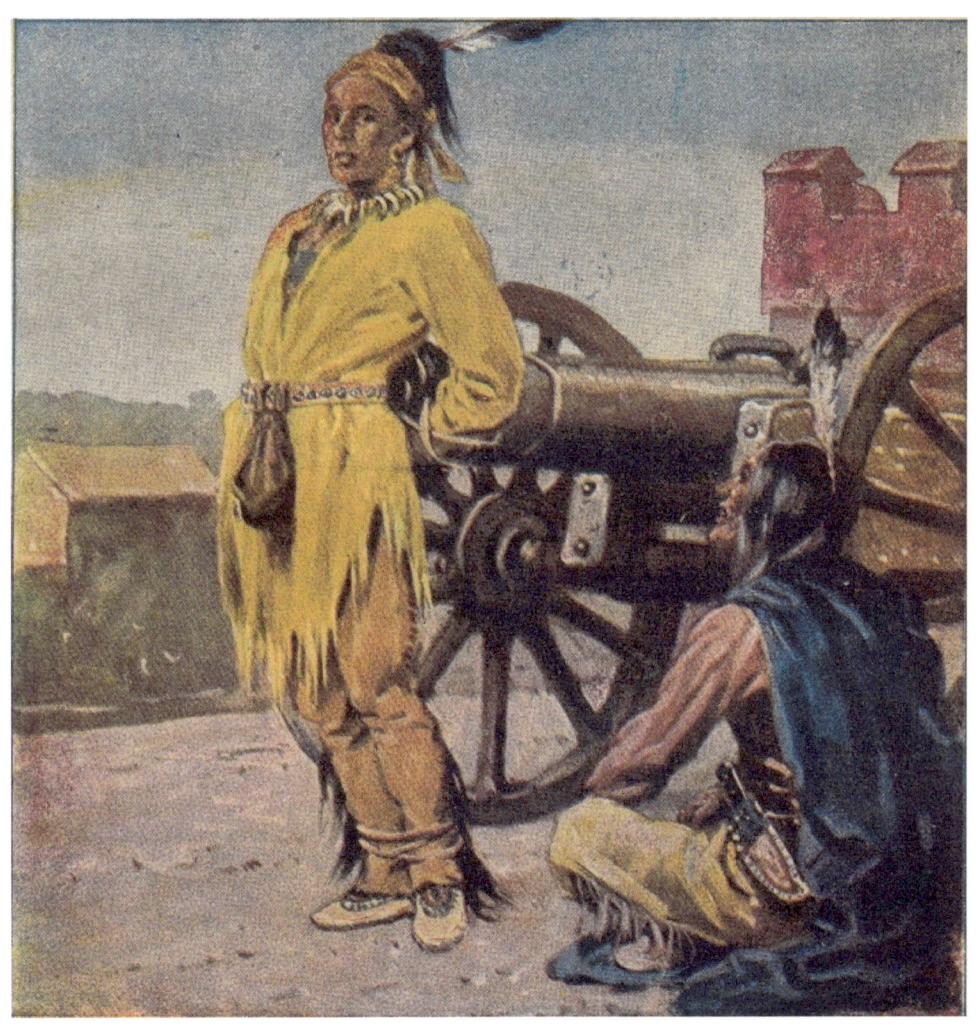

Mack-Wan el Invencible (Mack-Wan the Invincible) No. 4, 1933. El misterio de la grande piramide (Mystery of the Great Pyramid). Anonymous (José Canellas Casals), cover by Marc Farell.

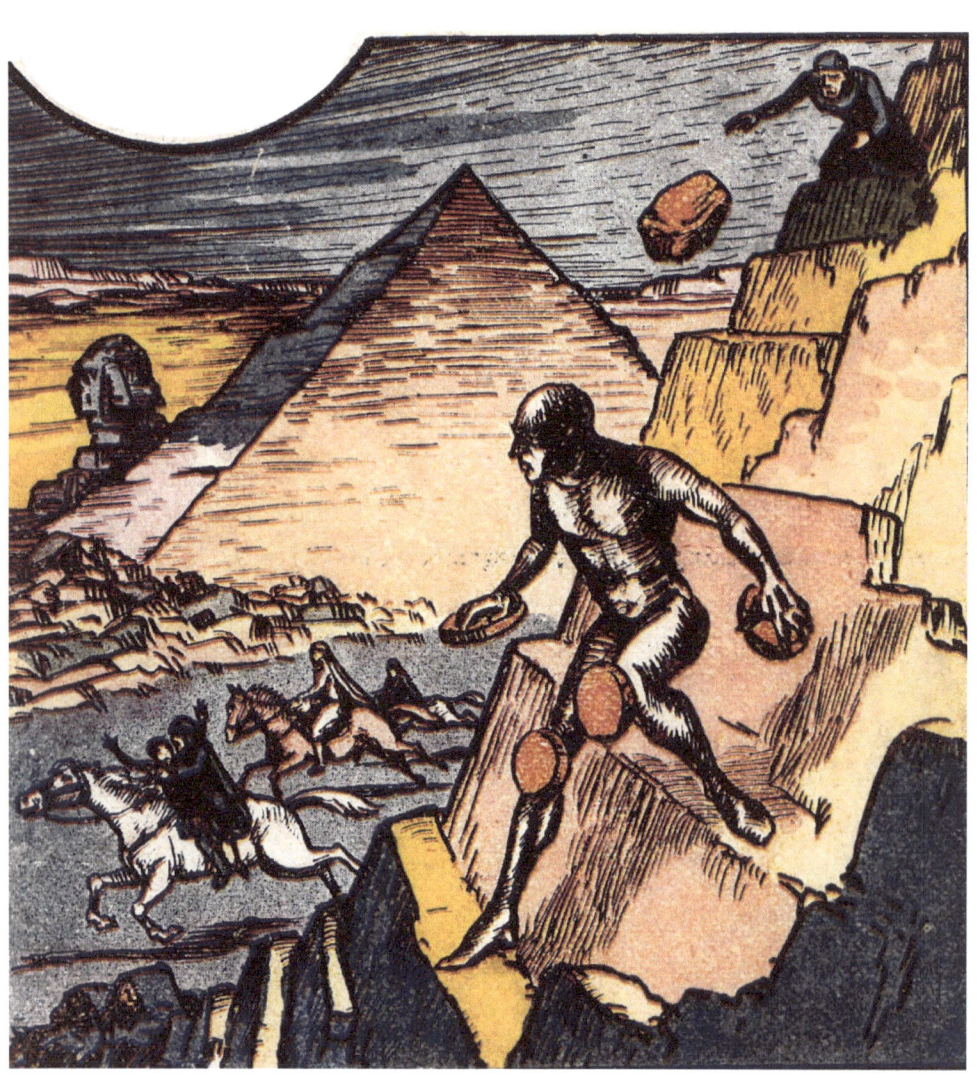

Ultimos Episodios de Nick Carter No. 59, circa 1920,
Una Victima de la magia (A Victim of Magic),
uncredited (probably Frederick Van Rensselaer Dey),
reprint of *New Nick Carter Weekly* No. 588, April 4,
1908.

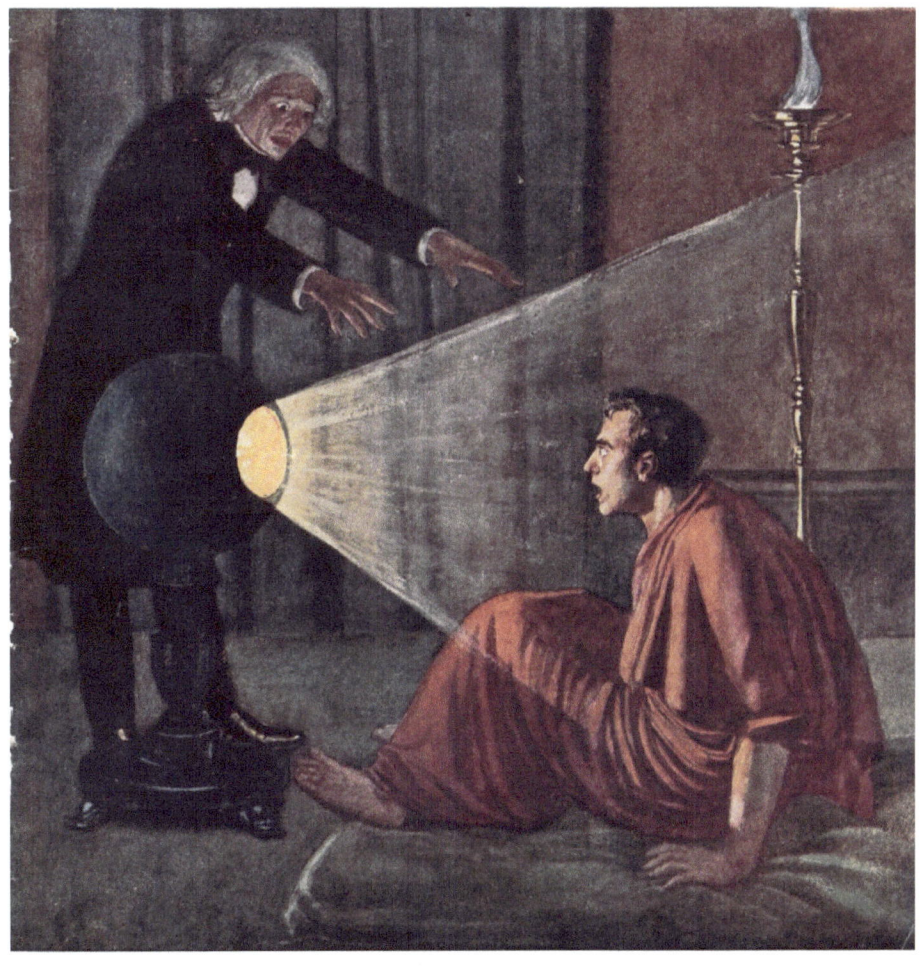

Rouges et Blancs (Reds and Whites) No. 1, 1913. Tungas, l'Otage Delaware (Tungas, the Delaware Hostage), from A. Eichler, a German publisher who printed magazines in France simultaneously. Released in Germany as *Der neue Lederstrumpf* (The New Leatherstocking).

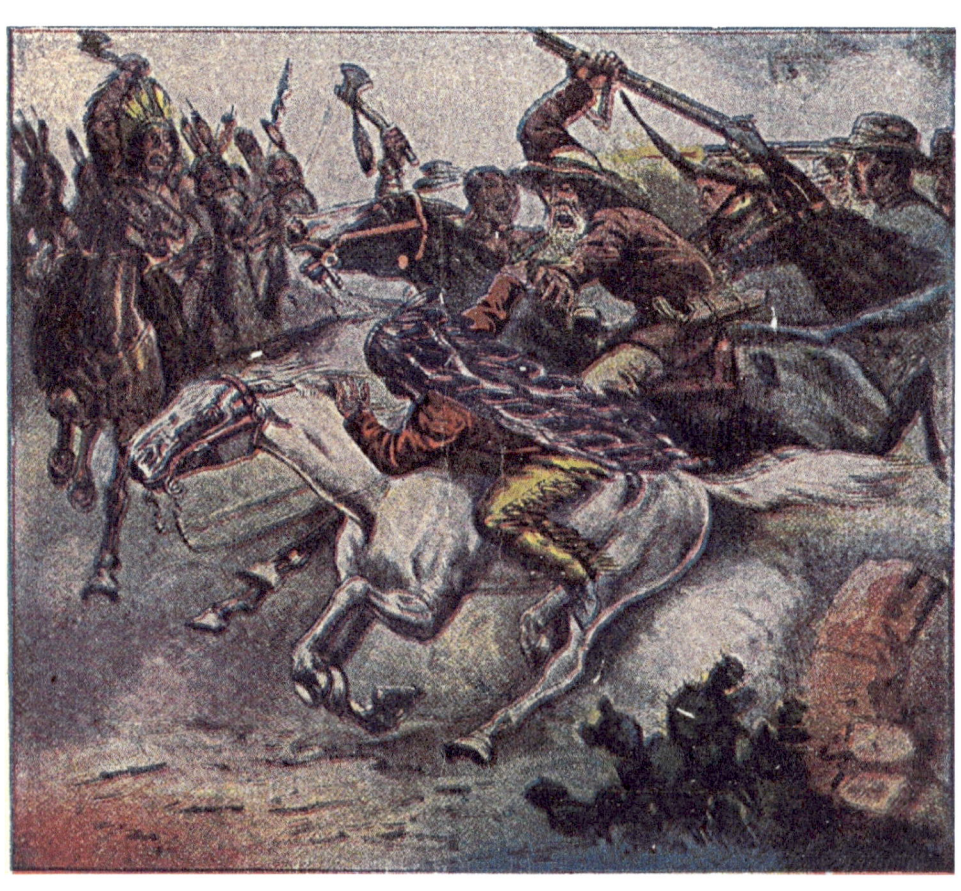

Trinket No. 14, circa 1920. Aventureas de un "Botones" (Adventures of a a Bellhop), El Suicidio de Sir Moses (The Suicide of...), by Eleme.

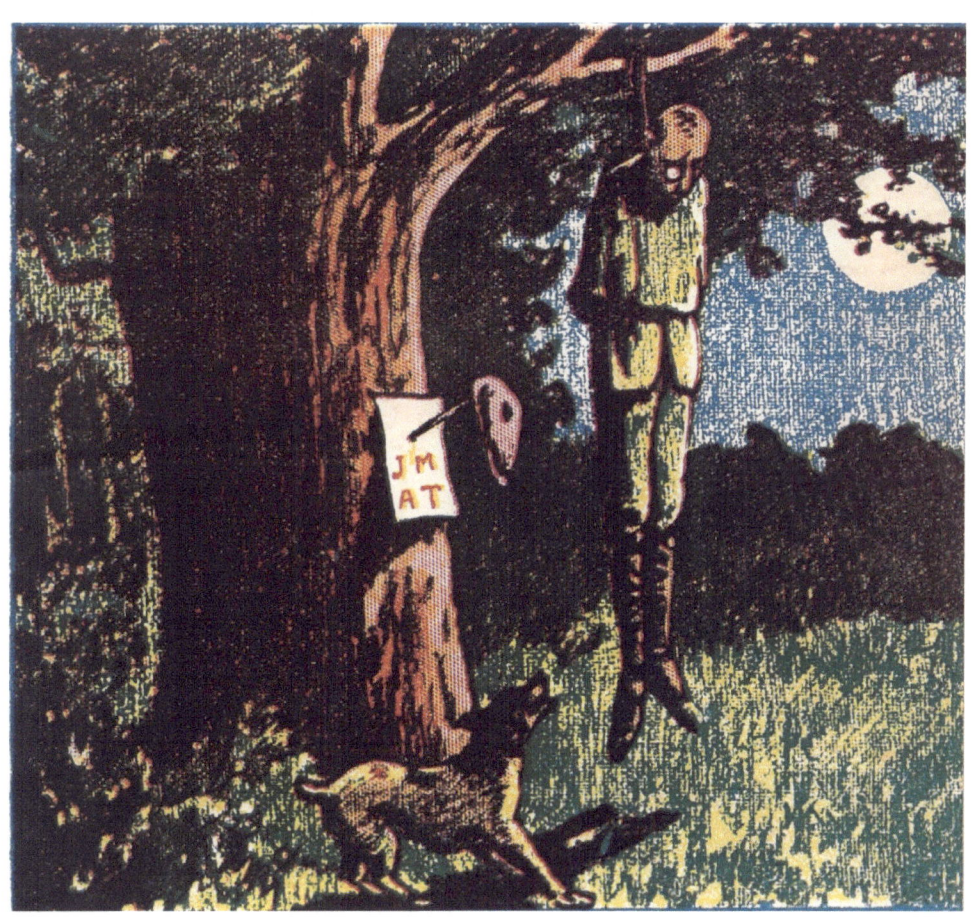

Nick Carter Lo Sterminatore del Malfattoi (Exterminator of Criminals) No. 13, May 4, 1930. I Misteri del telefono dell' Hudson (Mysteries of the Hudson Telephone), anonymous.

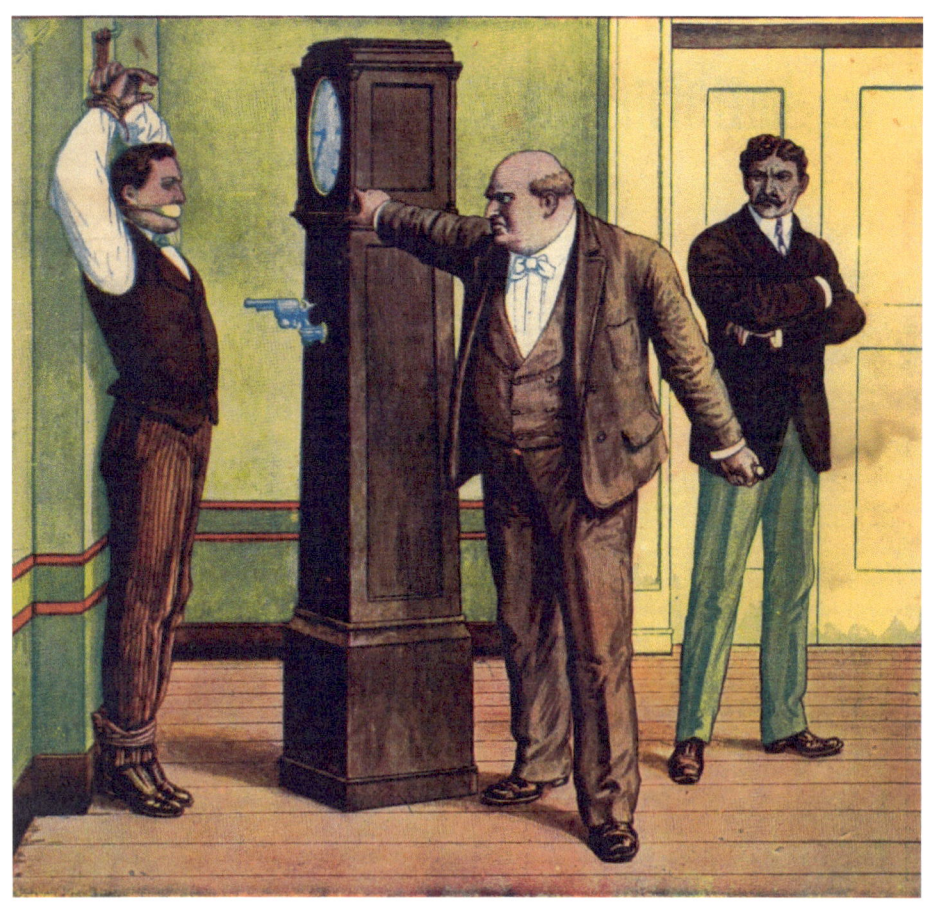

La Vuelta al Mundo de dos Pilletes (Two Scamps Around the World) No. 16, 1920s. La prision de "West-Gaol" (West-Jail Prison) by El Conde Henri de la Vaulx and Anrould Galopin, cover by Luis Palao.

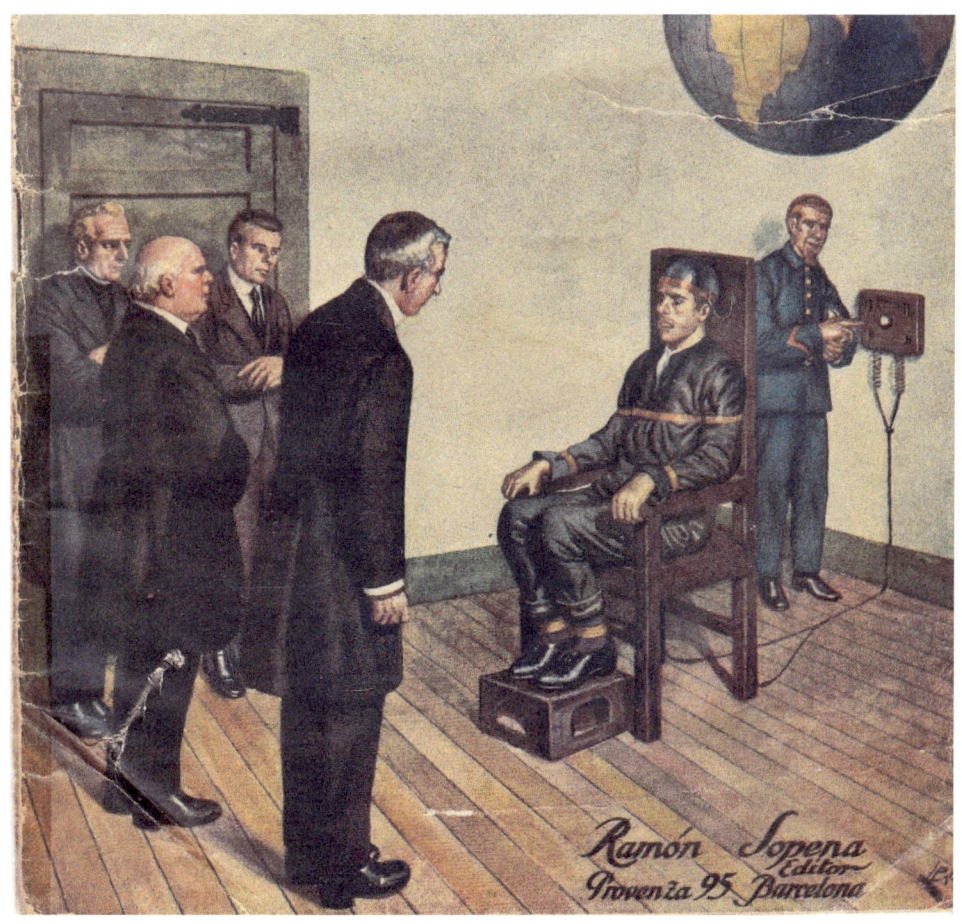

Buffalo Bill Aventuras Emocionantes No. 52, circa 1924. Los Cazadores Rojos (The Red Hunters), anonymous, cover by Luis Palao. Spanish reprint of *Buffalo Bill Stories* No. 102, April 25, 1903, Buffalo Bill in Dead Man's Swamp or Trailing the Red Man Hunters.

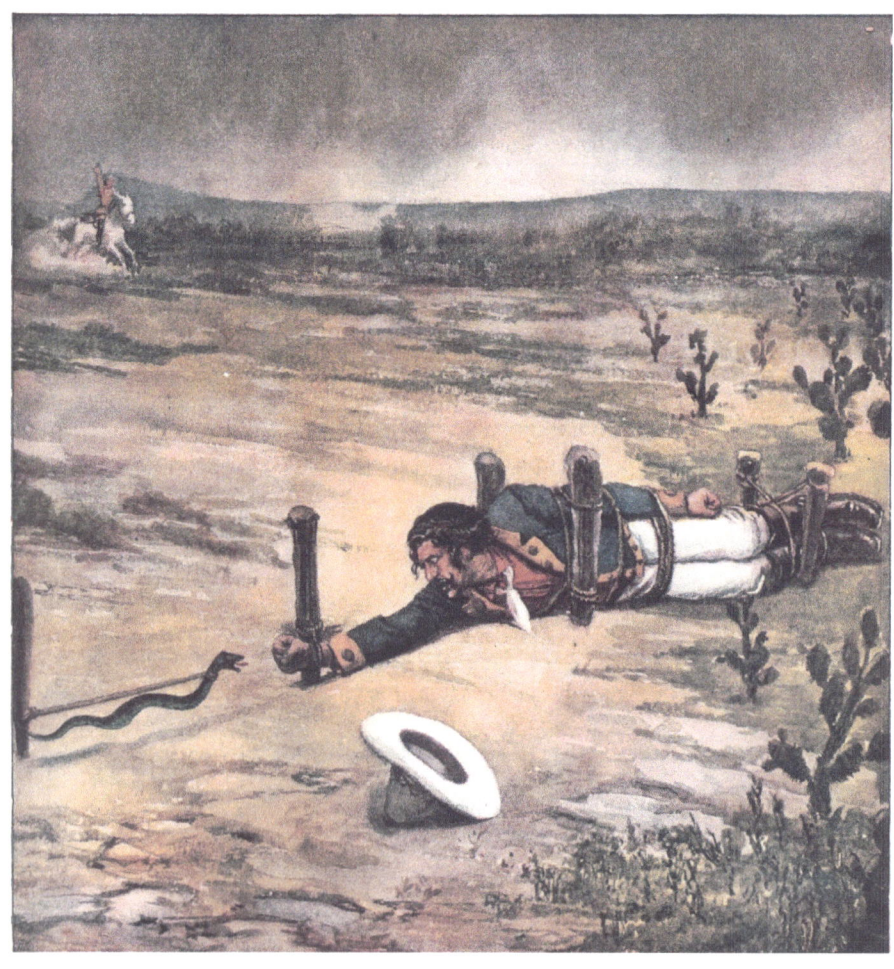

Tim Drake El hero del Far-West No. 15, circa 1926.
Bajo las Aguas del Rio (At the River's Bottom),
anonymous.

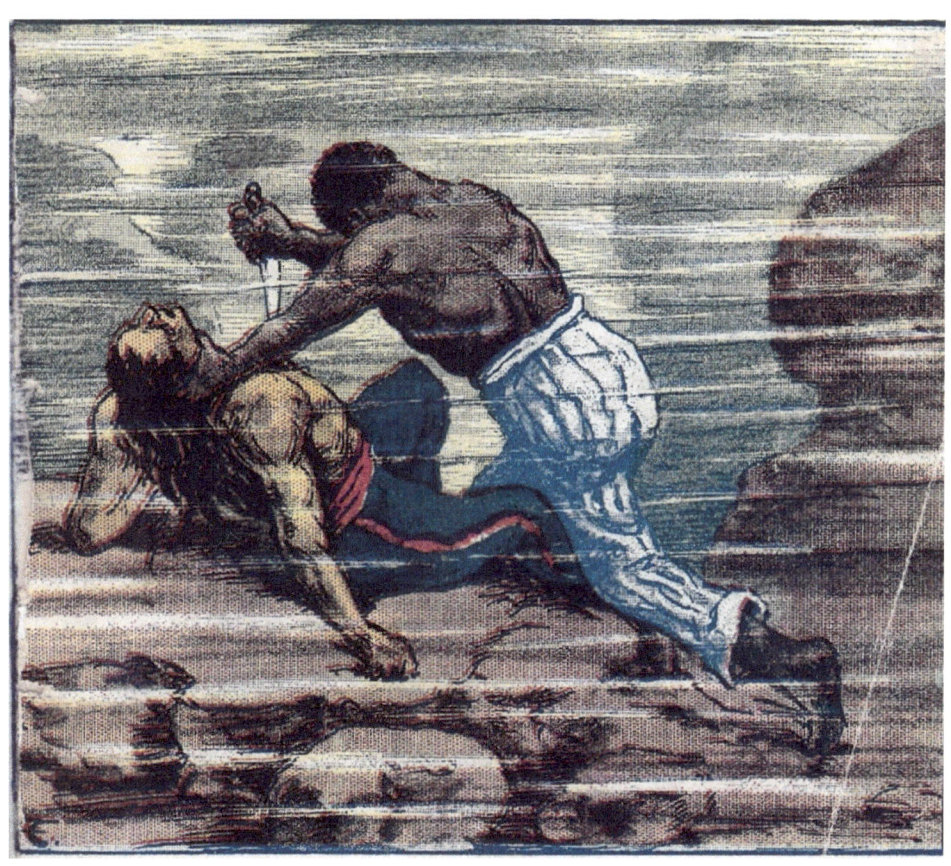

Ultimos Episodios de Nick Carter No. 77, circa 1920. Un Húron Acuatico, anonymous, new cover by Luis Palao. Reprint of *New Nick Carter Weekly* No. 616, October 17, 1908.

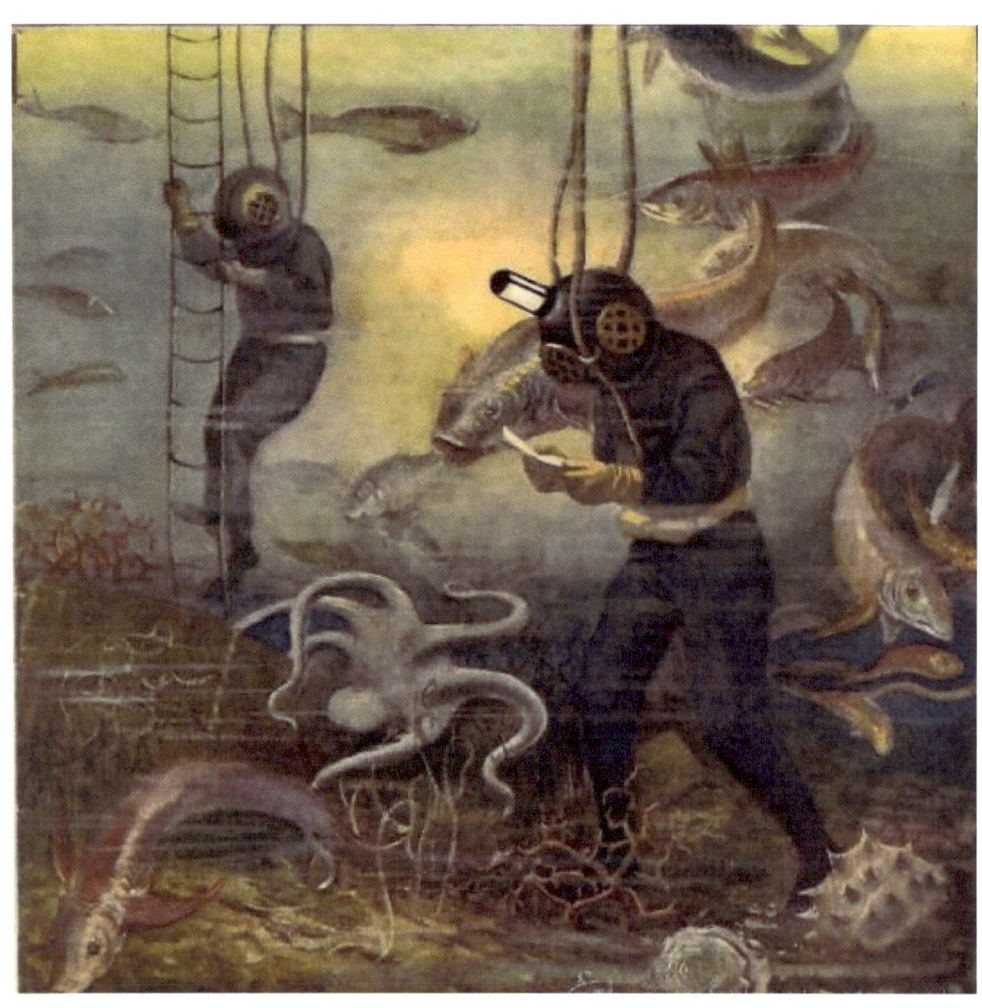

Buffalo Bill Aventuras Emocionantes (Buffalo Bill's Exciting Adventures) No. 50, 1924. La Calavera Animada (The Animated Skull), anonymous.

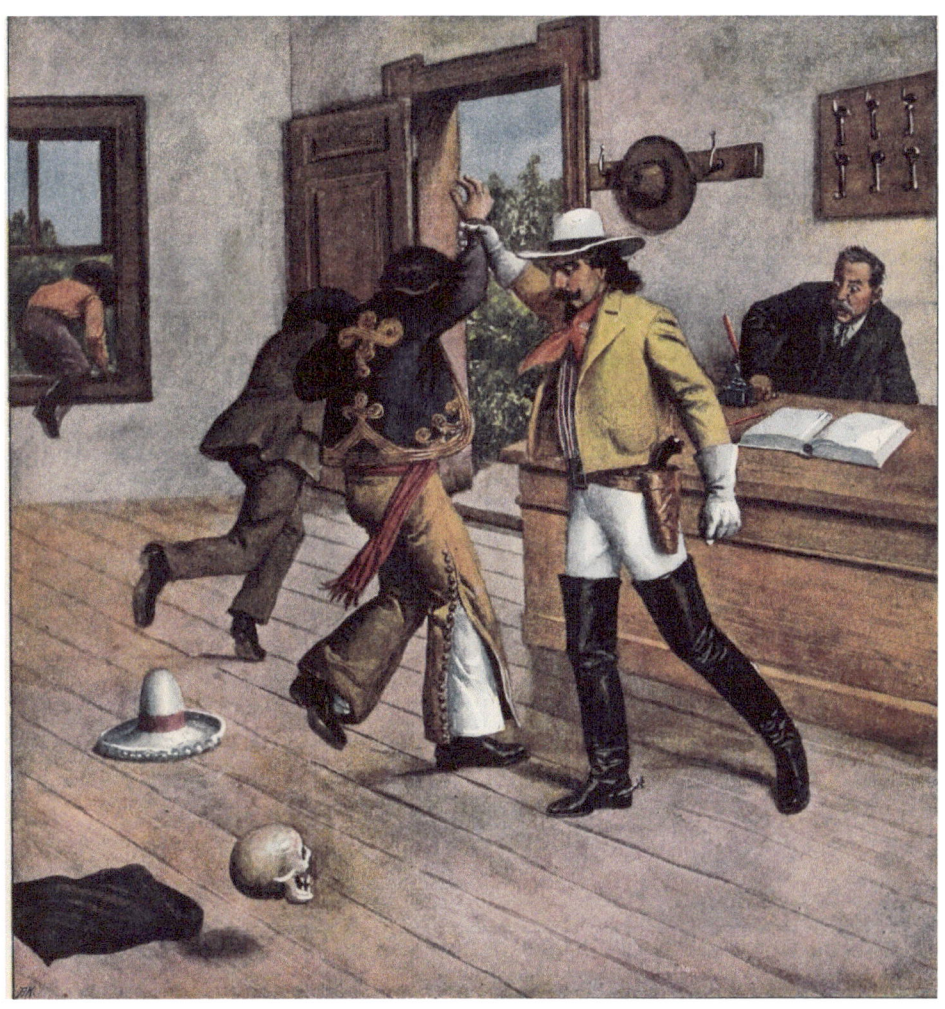

Tabú el Vengador de los Esclavos (Taboo The Avenger of Slaves) No. 33, circa 1930. El pastor Fredies (Pastor Fredies), anonymous.

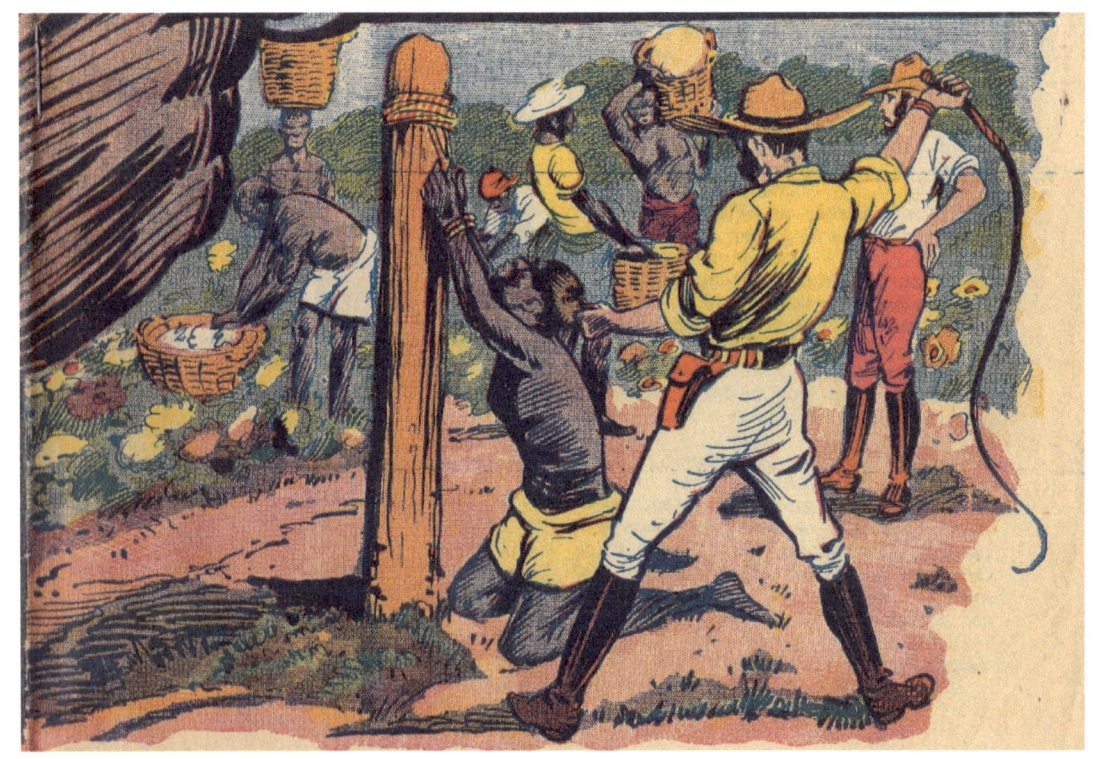

Ultimos Episodios de Nick Carter No. 17, 1930s. Los Secretos del Palacio Encantado (Secrets of the Enchanted Palace), anonymous (probably Frederick Van Rensselaer Dey). Reprints *Nick Carter Weekly* No. 565 with a new cover by Luis Palao.

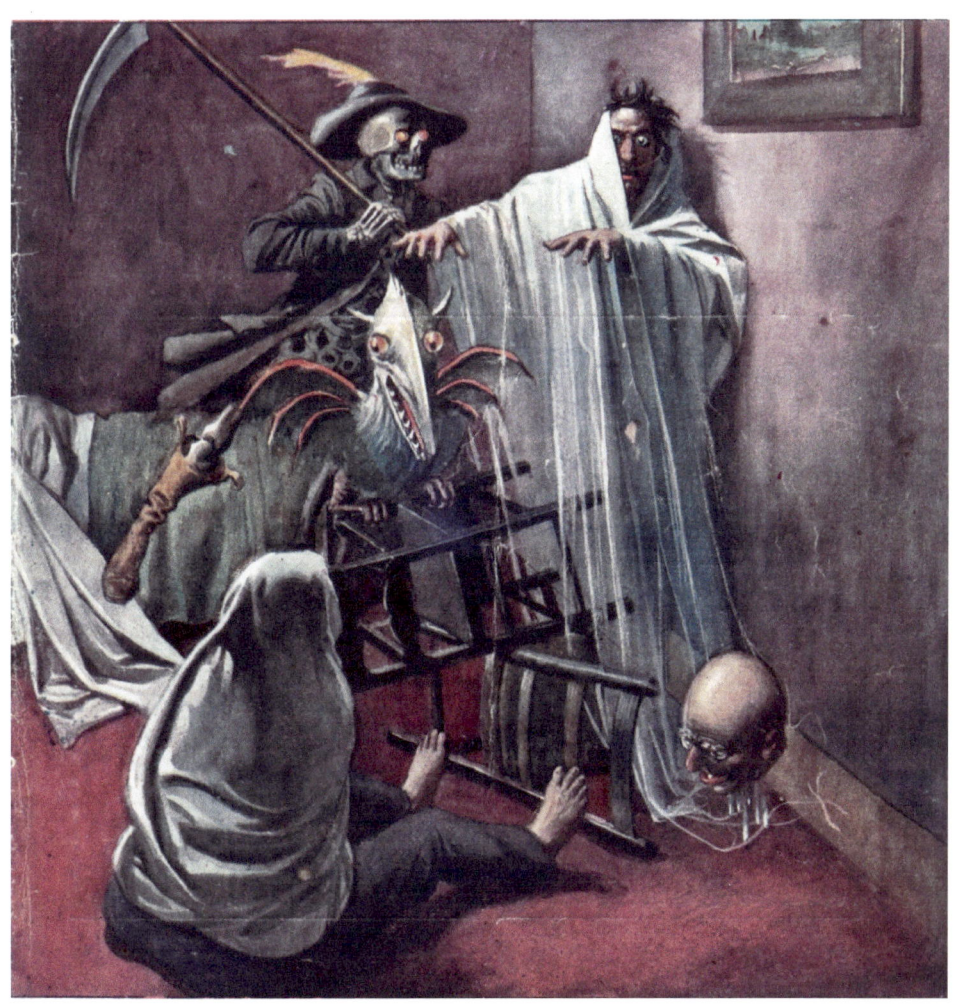

Coming soon:

The Witch Hunter's Wards

Joseph Lovece is a retired journalist and a collector of dime novels, pulp magazines and comic books. He lives in Florida.

www.ingramcontent.com/pod-product-compliance
Lightning Source LLC
Chambersburg PA
CBHW040857180526
45159CB00001B/449